FISHING THE DRY FLY

Dermot Wilson

Fishing the Dry Fly

Second edition

ADAM & CHARLES BLACK
LONDON

Second edition 1981
First published in this edition 1970
by A & C Black (Publishers) Ltd
35 Bedford Row, London WC1R 4JH

Originally published 1957
by Douglas Saunders with MacGibbon & Kee
under the title 'Dry-Fly Beginnings'

© 1981, 1970 Dermot Wilson

ISBN 0 7136 2134 6

Wilson, Dermot
Fishing the dry fly.—2nd ed.
1. Trout fishing—Great Britain
2. Fly-casting
I. Title
799.1.7   SH687
ISBN 0–7136–2134–6

Printed in Great Britain
by Redwood Burn Limited Trowbridge & Esher

CONTENTS

PHOTOGRAPHS

DEDICATION

To my Mother,

whose unselfishness has
made my fishing possible.

INTRODUCTION

This book about dry-fly fishing is intended mainly for beginners of all ages, though I hope that experienced dry-fly fishermen may also find a few things in it to interest them. It is essentially a collection of facts, and most of it was first published under the title *Dry-Fly Beginnings* some years ago. Now I have taken the opportunity to bring all the original facts up to date, and to include others which have been brought to light by fishermen or scientists since that time. I have tried to make them a set of simple but useful facts—the facts that have been most useful to me, anyway—about catching trout on a dry fly, about the trout and the flies themselves, and about dry-fly waters of various kinds, particularly the chalk-streams.

Dry-fly fishing, on the chalk-streams especially, has often been described as an art, and sometimes as a cult. People in fishing books always seem to be 'initiated into the mysteries of the dry fly', so that all sorts of secret and probably painful rites come to mind and they may get the idea that acceptance into the brotherhood of the élite can come to them only at the end of a very long process. If they take up dry-fly fishing, they may think they will have to pass through long years of apprenticeship during which they slowly approach Nirvana until at last, old and grey, they become high priests too late to do anything except sit on the bank talking about the Latin names of rare riverside insects.

What a lot of nonsense! Dry-fly fishing takes less time to learn than most other sports. Trout—let us whisper it softly—are very foolish creatures. After all, what do you actually do when you catch a trout on a dry fly from a chalk-stream? First you find a feeding fish—who gives away his presence by making rings on the surface of the water as he takes floating flies. Then, taking care not to frighten your trout, you throw over him a

bunch of feathers tied onto a hook, which he engulfs in mistake
for another fly. He does this with complete innocence although
sometimes your bunch of feathers looks very little like a fly at all.
Finally you drag a protesting trout into the net and feel very
proud of him. Over-simplification? Perhaps it is. But a good
many trout are caught almost as simply as this. Where, then,
is all the mystery? And where all the art?

Such art and mystery as do exist in dry-fly fishing probably
lie in being able to think like a trout. Some fishermen invariably
catch many more trout than others, and strangely enough they
are not necessarily the ones who are most skilful at casting,
playing and landing. But they do always seem to know quite
a bit about the ways in which trout live and feed and behave.
And they always seem to get twice as much pleasure out of their
sport as well. So, in writing this book, I have tried continually
to consider the *trout's* point of view.

Part One hurries rather quickly—as I think is right—over
the very elementary mechanism of dry-fly fishing. Part Two is
far more important, because it sets down some of the available
knowledge about trout and flies. Then Part Three puts a little
of this knowledge into practice, and Part Four rounds off the
volume with one long appendix and two short ones.

Appendix A is the long one. It is called *Questions of Tackle* and
gives the answers to the questions which seem to be uppermost
in fishermen's minds about the best tackle to use. The many
recent developments in tackle, some of which have tended to be
rather bewildering, make it worth going into the subject in
some detail. The appendix covers both dry-fly and wet-fly
tackle, so that the relationship between the two can be
explained, and because the information does not appear to
have been compiled before. Appendix B contains the knots a
dry-fly fisherman needs and Appendix C gives a few good
recipes for his wife.

I do not believe that I have passed very far beyond the stage
of a beginner myself. Has anyone? This book contains no
startling revelations to bring each and every trout inevitably to
the net. It simply aims to assemble and present the most
important and relevant known facts about trout and about flies.
Its object, above all else, is to relate dry-fly fishing as closely as

possible to the trout's way of life. I hope that in doing so it may be of some small use to people who enjoy dry-fly fishing, or who think they might enjoy it.

Nether Wallop Mill,
Stockbridge,
Hampshire.

ACKNOWLEDGEMENTS

It would take many pages for me to list the large number of fishing writers and friends who have contributed to my small knowledge of dry-fly fishing. But I should like to take this opportunity of thanking some of those who have helped me most directly with this book.

My thanks, then, are due to Lord Leslie, who encouraged the writing of it; to my wife Renée, who has not only allowed me to fish after marriage, but constantly puts me on my mettle by catching more trout than I do; to Miss Jackie Cox, who has tirelessly and patiently deciphered my handwriting and produced typescripts; to Dr. W. E. Frost, who has criticised and checked my biological facts about trout; and to the many people who have explained the technicalities of tackle to me, including Julian Mills, Alan Sharpe and Barrie Welham.

PART ONE

ELEMENTARY STEPS

Chapter 1

One Trout on a Dry Fly

There is only one secret in dry-fly fishing, which is to make an artificial fly float over a trout in such a way that it looks appetizing enough for him to swallow. All the gear that dry-fly fishermen have, and all the actions they go through, are merely intended to achieve this single aim. All their knowledge about insects, and all their different dry-fly patterns, just help to make the fly more appetizing—because the most appetizing fly to a trout is usually the one that looks most like the natural fly he is feeding on at the moment. Dry-fly fishermen are supposed, also, to creep and crawl around the river-bank on their bellies. The only point of this, when it is done—which is not so often as many people think—is to make sure that the trout is still there when the fly gets to him, instead of being frightened into the nearest weed-bed.

Obviously the right place for a dry-fly to be is near enough to a hungry trout for him to see it. The rod and line help to get the fly to the right place. In some places trout are nearly always hungry, usually because there is very little food in the water and they have to make the most of whatever they can find. Then they will often come up to any fly they catch sight of. But in most really good trout waters, where there is plenty of food and the fish are bigger and better-fed and much lazier, they tend to feed at the surface only at certain times of the day, when fairly large numbers of natural flies have appeared and are floating on the water.

Then the trout in lakes and reservoirs cruise around close to the surface, gulping down flies and making a little set of rippling rings every time they do so. This set of rings is called a rise. The trout in rivers take up positions near the surface and wait for the current to carry flies over them. They, too, leave rings behind them on the water when they swallow a fly. You should cast

1

your fly in the path of a cruising trout in still water, or a short way upstream of a stationary trout in a river. In the lake the trout will eventually come towards the fly and in the river the fly will eventually come to the trout, so long as it is cast accurately to him from downstream. It should always float towards him quite peacefully and naturally, at the pace of the stream itself.

Suppose, for instance, that you are on a trout-river and you see a trout rising over by the far bank, where two or three king-cups may be growing by the water's edge. He looks as if he is

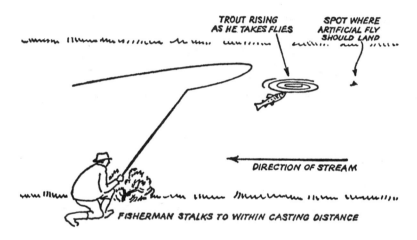

TROUT RISING AS HE TAKES FLIES

SPOT WHERE ARTIFICIAL FLY SHOULD LAND

DIRECTION OF STREAM

FISHERMAN STALKS TO WITHIN CASTING DISTANCE

feeding well, since every thirty seconds or so the rings of his rise show on the surface as he sucks in a floating insect. The first step of all, usually, is to decide which of your artificial flies is most likely to tempt him. So you have to watch him for a little, to find out what sort of natural insect he is feeding on so eagerly, or at any rate to make a pretty accurate guess. Flies can be seen on the water and several are floating down under the near bank—big, darkish flies with tall, sombre-coloured wings which at king-cup time, in April, can only mean that they are Large Dark Olives. Then, onto your 'cast' or 'leader'— the thin length of nylon which is connected to the end of your line—goes a nicely tied Rough Olive.

Now the fish has to be stalked. This has to be done from

downstream, since trout always face upstream. The whole idea is to get close enough to be able to reach him with the fly, yet not so close that you frighten him by your presence or by the waving of the rod. On some heavily-fished rivers trout are notoriously shy and you have to fish for them from a respectful distance; on other rivers they are far more innocent. If you intend to cast from a kneeling position—or if you are wading in the stream—you can probably get rather closer to your trout than if you try to cast standing high up on the bank. Fish feeding well are usually the easiest to approach. A trout who is rising quickly and unhesitatingly, grabbing every fly he can see, is often so concerned with his next mouthful that he will not take much notice of fishermen; a trout rising spasmodically is generally more alert and quicker to take fright.

Sometimes, when you can actually see a trout in clear water, you can tell that he is hungry even if there are no natural flies for him to rise to. A hungry trout, ready to feed on fly, usually lies fairly close to the surface. He will probably be keeping his position with quick, energetic flicks of his tail, rather than with slow, leisurely sweeps; he may, from time to time, veer a foot or two to one side so as to examine odd fragments brought down by the current, in the hope of finding food among them. There is a sort of electric look about him. He, too, will be more intent on his meal than on your approach, and you can usually reckon that he is a likely trout to catch.

Fish rising with cover close at hand—whether the cover consists of weeds, rocks or the river-bank—are often easier to approach than fish rising in open, unprotected stretches of water. They may feel that with cover nearby they have a quick escape-route from their enemies and can feed more confidently. At any rate, if I see a trout rising under the bank or right up against a weed-patch, I am inclined to bargain on getting a little closer up to him than I would otherwise. Perhaps for the same reason, trout in carriers or narrow streams will sometimes allow fishermen to come nearer to them than trout in broad rivers do.

There is an old fishing expression 'fine and far off', which may have cost fishermen a good many trout. Casting for a trout from farther away than is strictly necessary is a bad idea. The cast will be that much less delicate, and when you strike to drive the hook home, you will do it less well. It is always difficult to strike with a long length of line lying between the rod and the fish. The only man I know who can consistently hook fish at very long range is Charles Ritz. Most of us can't. There is really very little point in setting yourself exercises in long-distance casting if you can possibly help it.

Having decided from which spot you wish to cast for your trout, the next move is to get there. This may mean crawling or crouching for the last few yards if the trout in the river are particularly shy. And it may also mean making use of whatever cover there is on the bank in the way of vegetation. It is worth remembering that if you cast for a trout from in front of a bush, you may be even more invisible to him—because you do not show up against his skyline—than if you cast from behind it. Cover on the bank is an asset to stalking, but it has its disadvantages, too. Before casting, it is always well worth while looking behind to make sure that the line of the cast is clear of trees and bushes. All too often the cast or fly gets fouled-up in twigs, branches, tall thistles and so on, when a quick glance around could easily have avoided it. There is no better case of 'more haste, less speed' than in preparing to cast for the first time over a fish.

This is very true in another way, too. It is usually wise to treat your first cast purely as an experiment, and to drop it just behind the trout, instead of directly in front of him. A cast that falls short cannot possibly frighten him, but a cast that goes too far and shows him the line is bound to do so. Also, this preliminary cast tells you whether the *next* cast—which you hope will touch down neatly a few inches upstream of the trout—is going to be in any grave danger of 'dragging'.

'Drag' is one of the dry-fly fisherman's bugbears. An artificial fly should float downstream in exactly the same way as a natural fly. But when any part of the line or leader between rod and fly is carried along by the current faster than the fly itself, it pulls on the fly and drags it sideways across the surface. You may, for instance, be fishing for a trout rising in a quiet glide by the far bank, but between you and the far bank may be faster eddies. When these act upon the belly of the line the effect is very soon seen on the fly. It begins to skitter and skate across the top of the water, leaving a wake behind it.

Now no natural up-winged fly behaves like this. If a trout sees such a performance he will not take the fly and may well stop feeding. Even if the drag is not pronounced enough to cause a visible wake behind the fly, it may still make it float a little unnaturally, with the same effect on the trout. This invisible drag is responsible for many refused flies.

A fisherman can take certain steps to avoid drag when he has to, and these will be dealt with in the next chapter. But let us suppose for the moment that everything has been done perfectly. The fly is the right one. The trout has not been frightened during the stalk. Your cast has been accurate and there has been no drag. The sequel, in this case, should be quite the most exciting moment in dry-fly fishing—when the trout actually takes the fly. One second, there is the fly floating along. The next second it vanishes in front of your very eyes, having been sucked neatly and quickly beneath the surface. This is when you have to remember to strike.

The idea in striking is to raise the rod and tighten the line, deliberately but quite firmly—never hard enough to break the cast—so that you drive the hook home in the trout's mouth. ('Tighten' would be a better word than 'strike'.) But how often everyone tries to do just this, merely to find the fly sailing back overhead without having touched the trout at all! 'They're coming a bit short today' is the usual excuse.

But are they? If our fly is nearly the right one, but not quite, the trout may indeed come constantly short and never take it wholeheartedly. Often, however, the strike has merely been mis-timed. In shooting it is said that more birds are missed behind than in front. On the chalk-streams, it is an axiom that more fish are missed by striking too fast than too slow.

Many fishermen build up for themselves an elaborate rule for striking. When a fish takes, some say 'One thousand, two thousand, *three*—' and then strike. Others curb their impatience by chanting 'God save the *Queen*'.

None of these rules is a complete answer in itself, because all fish rise a little differently. I myself never pause consciously before striking. It is instinct, as much as anything, that tells you just when to strike. This is where a fisherman's feel of the situation can perhaps be compared with the 'hands' of a horseman. Sometimes you v. 'll find yourself missing fish after fish, and losing confidence steadily, so that you strike more and more wildly. But again, there will be days when you can do nothing wrong. Every time a trout rises to your fly, you know surely that you will hook him, and surely enough, every time you tighten on a fish the steel goes in fairly and squarely.

There is, however, one good guide for striking, other than instinct. Whenever a trout takes a fly he has to close his mouth at some stage. That is the time to strike. Think what a trout does as he rises. He lets the current carry him backwards and upwards till his nose meets the surface. Then he takes the fly. Then he forces himself down and upstream to his original place. While he is forcing himself down after rising, his mouth must be tight closed, otherwise it would offer too much resistance to the water. Strike then, and you are very likely to hook him. If you strike earlier, you *may* hook him, because the fly can still catch in his open mouth—but the chances are not nearly so good. If the strike comes later, he may well have opened his mouth again, either to breathe or to get rid of his last unwelcome mouthful.

Now a trout rising in fast water closes his mouth sooner, and gets back to his position more quickly, than a trout in slow water. If not, he would be carried some way downstream and have to make more effort to swim back. A large trout usually tackles a fly at a more leisurely speed than a smaller one. A trout coming up for a fly from deep down moves faster than a trout lying near the surface, since he has a greater distance to travel. This is why in hill-streams, where the current is swift, where the trout are small, and where they do not take up stations near the top of the water so frequently as in the slow chalk-streams, you always have to strike very quickly.

What happens next? Imagine that the strike has been successful. The rod is a-hoop, and a sizeable trout is making off towards the far bank as fast as he can go, diving deep and taking out line from the reel. A good sign. A well-hooked trout usually plays deep, while a lightly hooked fish tends to thrash around on the top of the water. Anyway, your heart is in your mouth. Even the most phlegmatic person can hardly remain calm and unruffled during the first nerve-racking run of a strong fit fish. A young girl, whom my family knew fairly well, acquired a stepmother several years ago—a cool, witty, self-collected and sophisticated woman of whom she was scared stiff. Nothing could ever shake the stepmother's self-possession— or so it seemed until father, daughter and stepmother all went on a fishing holiday to Scotland. On the first day the step-mother announced confidently that she needed no help from gillies or anyone; that she would find, hook, play and gaff her own salmon. So she walked off downstream. After an hour or two the girl followed her. She came upon her stepmother just as she had actually hooked a salmon, and to her surprise heard this unshakeable woman saying over and over again: 'Please-God-let-me-land-this-salmon-and-I-promise-I'll-be-a-good-girl-as-long-as-I-live. Please-God—.' The salmon was landed, and of course the stepmother and her stepdaughter then became the closest of close friends.

A trout is quite exciting enough, though he is smaller. If he is large enough to take out line, you may feel as if you have no control over him at all and there seems no earthly reason why you should ever land him. Playing a fish is not the most important part of dry-fly fishing, but a good few fish can be lost by bad playing. A fish has to tire himself out before he can be brought to the net. He can only do this against the tension you exert through the rod. This is one good reason for never, never losing contact with him if you can avoid it. If he runs towards you, you must recover the line by reeling in and take up the strain just as quickly as you can. Then he will tire soon. It has been shown that even a cross-channel swimmer can only last a very short time against the strain of a rod.

Another good reason for keeping up this constant contact with a trout is that although you may not be able to stop his rushes you can nearly always guide them. Left to himself, the trout may vanish into a clump of weeds or twirl the cast round a snag. The best way of turning him before he gets to one of these unpleasant places is to apply side-strain, which means pulling from the side with the rod held horizontally, rather than from the top. A trout swims by flexing his body sideways. So you can throw him off balance and change his course by pulling from the side. If you try walking towards a given point with someone tugging at you from the right or left, you will find it far less easy to keep your direction than if the tug is from straight behind.

There is a great deal to be said for the old golden rule of playing: 'Always keep your rod up'. The higher the rod-top is, the more control you have over your fish, because you can vary the tilt quickly in any direction to apply side-strain. Also the trout is less likely to break the cast, since the first force of his rushes will be absorbed by the bending of the rod. A trout should not really break the cast, ever. Or not unless he gets into the weed or around a snag. It is amazing how strong even a fine cast is. If you take your fly between your fingers and try to break your tackle by pulling against the spring of the rod, you will find it nearly impossible. Only a sharp jerk when the cast is attached to something firm will break it. Sometimes a break occurs through striking too vehemently. But normally it should never happen unless the cast is rotten or there is a faulty knot.

As a result it is sensible to treat the trout fairly roughly. Namby-pamby playing, when a trout is handled as if it were on the end of a gossamer thread, merely prolongs the agony for both parties concerned. If a fish is well hooked he will usually stay on despite any amount of bullying. If not, he will probably come off anyway. An old keeper who once taught me a great deal was so attached to this policy of 'treat 'em rough' that whenever I hooked a fish he used to shout: 'Hold 'un, sir; hold 'un! *Don't* let 'un run.' Sometimes he even used to put his hand on my reel to stop a large fish from taking out line. It was surprising how seldom we lost a fish. Now I think he carried matters a little too far. It is highly dangerous to put your hand on the reel when a fish is actually running. If he wants line, he should usually be indulged. But nevertheless, it is feasible and wise and humane to tire a fish quickly, to play him and not play with him.

Unfortunately, a hooked trout manages to bury himself in a weed-bed only too frequently. Many people believe—and it seems perfectly possible to believe it oneself—that when he does this he often hangs on to the weed with his mouth. You can haul at him with the rod as long as you like but you will seldom shift him. The best thing to do is to try handlining. Let out several yards of line from the reel until there is a long length of slack between you and the trout. Then pick up the line *between* the rod-tip and the trout so that you have a direct pull on your fish. But do not pull. Pluck gently. At the first pluck, you will feel nothing but the dead weight of the weed. At the third or fourth pluck you will feel something alive at the end. This is the trout beginning to kick free. After a few more plucks the fish will abandon the weed and come into open water. Then drop the line quickly, reel in the slack and go on playing the trout. For some reason, trout always seem to react in the right way to this plucking, and it is seldom long before they loosen their hold on the weed and come clear.

When the trout is tired out he can be landed. It may be relevant to state here a purely personal prejudice about landing-nets. I do hate the V-shaped collapsible ones that are so convenient to pack into suitcases. I am sure you often pay dearly for the convenience later, perhaps just when you want to land the best trout of your day. The mesh of the net may become inextricably entangled in the collapsed part of the 'V' and all the shaking and swearing in the world will not uncollapse it. One more disadvantage is that owing to the shape of the net you have to steer your fish in a certain direction over it to make use of its full width. Nor can you feel around in weed with it.

For myself, I infinitely prefer a round rigid frame. If you fish from a high bank the handle should be quite long—or telescopic—but if you fish from a low bank or wade, it can be much shorter. A net like this seldom lets you down. You can bring your fish into it from any angle or direction. And if by any chance a trout fails to come out of the weeds when you pluck the line, a net with a solid frame allows you to go and probe around for him in the weed-bed.

When you land a trout, it is wise not to swoop or scoop at him with the landing-net. You may hit the cast and break it, or knock him off the hook, or frighten him into making a last plunge which may gain him his freedom. All landing should be carried out with deliberate care. First, unless you are wading, you have to choose a spot on the bank where you can stand firmly, and where your net can reach the water easily. The water around should be clear of weeds and snags if possible.

Then you have to guide the trout towards this spot. In order not to tie yourself into knots, hold the rod in your upstream hand and the net in your downstream hand. These will be the right hand or left hand according to which bank of the river you are on. Sink the net gently a few inches beneath the water. Keep low while you are doing it, for the less a trout sees of you the less likely he will be to get panicky and kick loose. Then draw the beaten trout quietly over the net, without moving the net itself until the moment when you can simply lift it up from the water with your trout inside it.

So there he is on the bank at last. He is a gleaming prize and every lovely ounce of him is all yours. Let us hope that he is fat as butter, with the small head and thick body of a fit fish in tip-top condition. Your heart will probably smite you as you look at him, and you will feel an urge to put him back in the river before he dies. If you can bear to do it so much the better. But baser nature is likely to prevail—and so long as your trout is appreciated at table, that is not at all an unfitting end for him. A family that enjoys trout is a considerable asset to any fisherman—for there is something of the hunter in all of us.

That particular trout was rising steadily and was easy to spot. You knew exactly where he was. You were in fact 'fishing the rise'—which means casting only for fish you see feeding. 'Fishing the water' means casting where you think fish *may* be feeding. You will normally 'fish the rise' on streams such as southern chalk-streams, which are rich in natural fly-life, and where you hope to see plenty of fish rising. But on many other streams, where there are fewer flies and fewer signs of trout on the feed, you will 'fish the water'. The trout may well rise readily when and if they see a fly—but you have to guess where they are.

And this won't be blind guesswork. Using your experience of trout and their habits, you will find yourself thinking where *you* would lie if you happened to be a trout. Soon your own intuition will be telling you where to put each cast, and you will more and more often have the satisfaction of being right. And predicting the 'lie' of a trout successfully is one of the greatest rewards of dry-fly fishing. Out goes your fly towards that smooth glide under an overhanging branch. It alights softly, floats down daintily. You can see it standing up proudly. on its hackles—until suddenly it disappears in the middle of a series of those breath-taking rings. 'I *thought* so', you can say rather smugly, as you tighten on a trout.

Then there is still-water fly fishing. New reservoirs, man-made expanses of still water, are providing more opportunities for trout fishing every year. Wet flies and 'lures' account for many trout. But so do dry flies and 'nymphs'. Again you can 'fish the rise' or 'fish the water'—remembering always that trout in still water keep on the move, since there is no current to bring food to them.

Wherever you fish the dry fly, you will be able to enjoy the thrill of actually seeing the trout take your fly. Other forms of fishing bring their own rewards. But this—this one moment of watching the fly fulfill its purpose of deception—is the dry-fly fisherman's unique privilege.

Chapter 2

Casting Principles

If you look at a rising trout hovering just below the surface, he may remind you a little of a lightweight boxer. He usually feints from one side to the other, stemming the current with deft movements of his fins, body and tail. Though he keeps a vigilant watch all around him for most of the time, his eyes are mainly directed forwards and upwards so that he can catch an early view of any surface-food that floats within his reach. Every now and again a fly dances down towards him on the top of the water. Then he tilts his head and shoulders up. The current gently takes charge of him, lifts him in the water and carries him backwards until his nose meets the little insect. The fly vanishes. The trout forces his head down again, swims back to his old place and leaves behind him only a series of ever-widening rings.

This is the sort of trout you can catch with the dry-fly, and now, when he is feeding on flies, is just the right moment. But first, of course, you have to be able to cast the fly. How long does it take to learn how to cast? Probably not more than about ten or twelve hours. If you have never cast a fly before in your life, and you lay aside two half-hours a day to practise it, you should easily be able to catch a trout in a chalk-stream inside a fortnight. You may not be an expert by then. When you try to cast into a stiff breeze you may get into one of those tangles that lead fly-fishermen so frequently to fall into blasphemy. You may cast fairly short distances only. Your wrist may begin to ache after a little. But you will be able to catch trout, and these matters will all right themselves quickly. The action of casting is a completely new experience for the muscles concerned, and until they become used to it they tend to protest and make heavy weather of the whole affair. Soon the action will become almost automatic and even a long line will go out smoothly.

No one, I think, has ever learned to cast properly out of a book. Nothing in the world can replace personal guidance here. The rhythm of casting is very different from swinging a golf-club, wielding a cricket-bat, cracking a whip or anything else. It is not really difficult but it is entirely unique, and unless you discover the feel of it at the outset, from someone who knows how to cast, you are liable to make the mistake of relating it to something you have done before. Then you are quite likely to go wrong.

So it is nearly always best, right at the outset, to find a friend who is prepared to give up a little time to passing on his own knowledge, or a professional who can give good lessons. Here are one or two hints, however, which may help to explain how casting works.

There are several separate styles of casting, each with its enthusiasts. They do not, however, differ from each other tremendously. They are all designed to make the fly do the same thing, so to understand the principles is more important than worrying about style.

It will help if you try to think of the *fly* on the end of the line and not merely of the rod itself. In most ball-games the object is to make the bat, racquet or club meet the ball at the correct angle with the correct force. Footwork, body-work, arm-work and hand-work all culminate at the end of the weapon. Casting a fly is another sort of thing altogether. Here, the rod is only a means to an end. It is used as a form of remote control to manipulate a length of line, and the item of equipment that really matters is the fly moving through the air several yards away. Waving a rod by itself does no good— it is the effect of the rod on the line and fly that makes a good cast or a bad cast.

The actual force a fisherman puts into casting is a good deal less important than the timing. He does not really cast the fly at all. The rod does. The spring in the rod gives the line its impetus. The fisherman merely controls the rod and helps it to do its work. When you were at school, did you ever flick those little balls of blotting-paper across your classroom with a ruler? If you remember, it was the released tension in the ruler that sent them flying so far—much farther than you could ever have thrown them by yourself without a ruler. The ruler had to be bent back to build up tension before it would flick forward successfully.

A rod works in very much the same way. It is the released

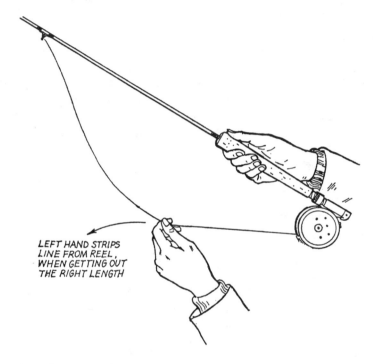

LEFT HAND STRIPS
LINE FROM REEL,
WHEN GETTING OUT
THE RIGHT LENGTH

tension that propels the line. And the rod-tip—just like the top of the ruler—has to be flexed (or bent) to develop this tension. But whereas you used to bend the top of the ruler with your hand, the rod-tip is bent by the *weight of the line*.

Each complete cast consists of a backward cast—or back-cast —and a forward cast. As the rod is lifted for the back-cast, it is bent by the weight of the line in front of you. This develops tension in the rod to propel the line backwards. Unless the rod does bend like this, it won't send the line back properly.

The same principle applies to the forward cast—but here

the rod bends against the weight of the line *behind*. It is vital to remember that the rod has to do this. It explains one great truth about casting—that the back-cast is just as important as the forward cast. Unless the line goes well out behind, the rod won't flex when you bring it forward—and then the line won't go out in front.

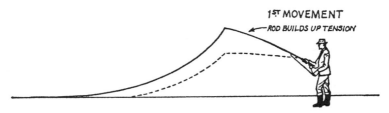

Let us take the back-cast and the forward cast in turn. Each of these consists of two movements that merge quickly into one another—the first movement building up tension in the rod, and the second movement using the tension to propel the line.

Suppose you are standing on a river bank, or on a lawn, with your rod in your hand, correctly gripped, and with your

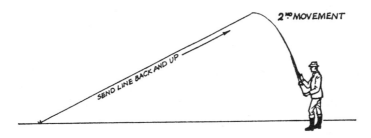

line stretched out in front of you, either on the water or on the grass. The rod is pointing straight forwards, parallel to the ground. Your line must be stretched straight out—if it is to act immediately on the rod-tip. The first movement of the backward cast, then, is to raise the rod-tip slowly and gently. Before the rod overcomes the inertia of the line—before the line begins to move at all, in fact—the rod-tip will bend down a little.

This is the building up of the tension, the equivalent of bending back the ruler. As soon as you feel the line starting to gather speed, increase the strength of the action smoothly but very quickly. Using mainly your forearm—rather than your wrist—drive the line backwards and upwards. That, the second movement, is the same as actually flicking the ball of blotting-paper.

The whole force of the movement here should be directed into sending the line back and *up*. If the line travels straight back towards a spot no higher than the fisherman himself, he is likely to find his fly trying to hit him fair and square in the face. Even if the fly misses him the line will probably fall downwards to become entangled in the grass at his back before he can begin the forward cast. One good idea when you practise casting is to rig up a clothes-line behind you, five or six feet high.

Back and up. Always remember the 'up'. It is one of the things that newcomers to casting always find most difficult. Here are two hints about it. First, if the line is to travel back and up, so must the rod-tip. It is not a bad idea to watch the rod-tip occasionally while you are learning to cast. So long as it is travelling upwards, it will be sending the line upwards, but if you bring it too far back, it will let the line drop down. Try not to bring it back far beyond the vertical—that is, to a point above and only slightly behind your right shoulder.

Second, keep your wrist stiff until the very end of the back-cast. If you bend or 'break' your wrist too early, the rod-tip will begin going back instead of back and up. And the result, again, will be that the line starts falling behind you. Do all you can to keep your back-cast high.

Now for the forward cast. After you have driven the line backwards and upwards, pause. It is important to pause momentarily at this point. The purpose of the pause is to allow the line to stretch out behind you so that when you bring the rod forward again, the weight of the line behind will bend back the rod-tip. This is how tension is built up for the forward cast. While you pause you can let the rod-tip 'drift' a little further back—to give you more power when the time comes to push the line out in front.

How long should you pause? It will depend largely on the 'bendiness' of your rod and on the length of line beyond the rod-tip. The more flexible your rod, the longer it will take

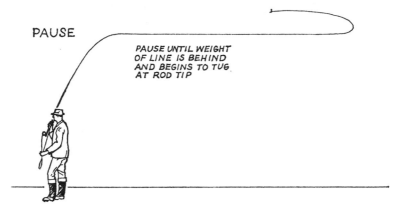

PAUSE

PAUSE UNTIL WEIGHT
OF LINE IS BEHIND
AND BEGINS TO TUG
AT ROD TIP

to develop and release tension. And the more line you have 'aerialised', the more time you have to allow for the pause.

The important thing is to pause until you know that the main weight of the line is behind you—it will tug slightly at

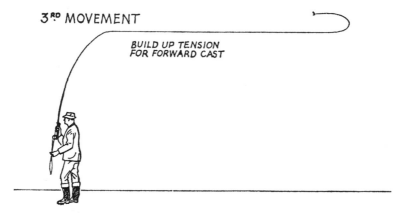

3ᴿᴰ MOVEMENT

BUILD UP TENSION
FOR FORWARD CAST

the rod-tip—and until you can feel that it will soon lose its backwards impetus and start falling.

While the line still has a little backwards impetus left in it, begin the forward cast. You will soon be able to tell when the exact moment has come. This question of timing is three-quarters of the secret in learning how to cast. When the moment arrives, start the forward movement fairly slowly again, building up tension against the weight of the line behind, but speeding it up very quickly indeed—using both wrist and forearm—so that the rod propels the line out forcefully in front of you. Aim for a point two or three feet above water-level. This action has sometimes been aptly described as 'knocking a nail into a tree on the opposite bank.' The line should not be cast *onto* the water—but into the air above the water. It must have time to straighten out, so that the fly can fall feather-light of its own accord on to the surface.

COMPLETION OF 4TH MOVEMENT

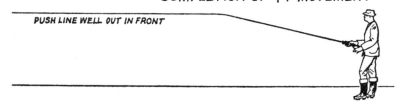

PUSH LINE WELL OUT IN FRONT

This is a description of one single cast from the time you start to lift the fly from the water to the time it settles there once more. When you actually fish for trout, you usually do a certain amount of 'false casting'. You cast the fly backwards and forwards in the air without allowing it to drop on the water. This is useful for several reasons. False casting dries the fly so that it floats, allows you to get out line, and helps you to judge distance as well. You can see just where your fly is going to fall when you eventually decide to drop it.

Do not let me leave the impression here that all the movements in casting are completely separated from one another. This is not so. There may be a distinct pause between the backward and forward cast, but the two movements in each —the building-up-tension movement and the sharper pushing or pulling movement—always blend smoothly into each other.

Finally, what does your left hand do? This hasn't been covered yet, and it is not essential to the main task of getting the rod to propel the line and fly. But your left hand still has an important part to play. While your right hand controls the *rod*, your left hand controls the *line*—holding it between the reel and the bottom ring of the rod. You use it to strip line out from the reel in preparation for casting. Then, while you are false casting, you can use it to pull or 'haul' at the line so as to increase line-speed. And last of all, you can use it to release the line at the end of your final cast—so that a few more yards will 'shoot' through the rod-rings for extra distance.

These, however, are only elaborations on a basic principle. At the outset the action of casting may well seem strange. The rod may seem a decidedly unwieldy implement while the line appears to take on a life of its own. As for the fly, it will probably show an aptitude for getting hooked into practically anything except trout. Then, after a week or so, the entire operation begins to fit together. The backward cast is seen to be just as important as the forward cast. (Unless the line goes really well out behind, it will never go well out in front). The body, arm, wrist, hand, rod, line, cast and fly all suddenly become part of a whole. Each does its own fair share of the work and no more. Casting, all at once, becomes effortless.

It is really amazing how little effort is needed to cast even a long line, once the timing and co-ordination come easily. Whereas at one time you may have found it necessary to give up casting practice after only half an hour, because your arm and wrist began to cry out for a sling, you now suddenly discover you can cast for hours without feeling tired. Also you can master quickly most of the more advanced tricks of casting—tricks like stretching out line against wind, casting backhand, casting underhand, or shooting line—because they are all variations of the same basic theme. The delicate dropping of a fly within a distant square foot of water, a feat that seemed almost miraculous once, becomes a mere matter of course in a very short time.

Good casting is not only a matter of distance. Good 'presenta-tion' is frequently, perhaps even usually, just as important or more so. Good presentation is the skill of making line, leader and fly fall gently on the water, all in a straight line, and exactly where you want them. If they do not fall straight, the trout may catch sight of the line. And when you strike, contact will be too slow. Indeed the value of casting a very long way is all too often over-rated. It can certainly be useful on some reservoirs where fish lie far out. But even on those reservoirs it is probable that more trout are caught within a distance of fifteen yards than outside it. A badly-presented fly—particularly a dry fly—will very, very seldom be taken by a trout. And the farther you try to cast, the more difficult you will find it to present a fly really well.

To present a fly well against a wind is never easy. Brute force doesn't help a great deal. If you try to overcome a wind merely by casting harder, you may succeed in driving out the line but you will not get over the real difficulty, which is that the lighter leader and fly will be blown back towards you. The way to avoid this is certainly not to strain at your casting.

When faced by a wind, try cutting your line down on to the water instead of aiming into the air above it. Then the wind has less time in which to affect the fly. And if you pull a little line *back* through the rings with your left hand, this helps to straighten out the leader. With some trial and error you will soon be able to cast into a fair breeze. A howling headwind, unfortunately, can sometimes make good casting virtually impossible unless you discover a sheltered spot or some stretch of the river where the wind is behind you.

Then there are certain ways in which casting can minimise the chance of drag. Drag, if you remember, is set up when the line is swept downstream faster than the fly and begins pulling the fly sideways across the surface. A very accurate cast, which puts the fly only a few inches upstream of the trout, sometimes prevents drag, when it might otherwise have happened. By the time the fly reaches the trout the belly of the line has not yet had an opportunity to become a nuisance.

But sometimes other measures are needed. Where the set of the current is really inconvenient, drag may start almost immediately. In these circumstances you should throw a deliberately crooked line. People who are finding out how to cast often become a little confused here, and no-one can blame them. First of all they learn how to throw a nice straight line; then, apparently, they are told to forget all about it and start doing the opposite. Nevertheless, where there is any fear of drag, an absolutely straight line can be a liability. The current may begin to set up drag as soon as the line and fly hit the water. The best sort of cast, when you meet this situation, is one that makes the line land in a curve or zigzag on the surface.

If, for instance, you jerk or wriggle the rod-tip right at the end of your cast just before the fly drops, the line, too, will fall in a series of wiggles. The current has to straighten them out before it can drag the fly. So you gain a certain amount of time during which you hope that the fly will pass over the fish and be firmly taken. Putting an upstream curve into the line, as it lands on the water, is another useful accomplishment, and not too hard to learn. But these accomplishments—which in any case apply only to rivers and not to still water—all come into the category of 'advanced casting' and you can catch plenty of trout without them.

Good casting is a pleasure in itself. It is what attracts many people to flyfishing. I know of at least one fisherman who casts beautifully but who has a habit of seldom leaving his fly long enough on the water for trout to take it. He is fully aware of this. 'I know I'd catch many more trout if I left it floating longer', he says, 'but then I wouldn't be able to cast so often, would I'?

Chapter 3

Equipment

Dry-fly tackle, and indeed fly tackle in general, has changed a good deal since the 'classic' writings of Halford and Skues a couple of generations or so ago. Improved processes of manufacture, and better designs as well, have allowed cane rods to be shorter and lighter for their power. Fibreglass, as a material for rod-building, has created its own revolution. Plastic floating lines have made the task of greasing a silk line unnecessary, but they have not been an unmixed blessing. Nylon has replaced silkworm gut as the most convenient material for casts or 'leaders'. And there have been many other changes.

All these developments have tended to make tackle more complicated and more specialised. New technical terms—such as 'fast tip action' to describe a rod—have been widely used, but perhaps not so widely understood. How many people really know the advantages and disadvantages of a 'forward-taper' line? And although many of the developments have been in specialised fields—for tournament casting or reservoir fishing, for instance—they have sometimes been taken up for 'ordinary' purposes. Then they often cause disappointment.

It is because of this that a detailed Appendix about tackle has been included at the end of this book. In it I hope you will find some information about the different materials used for making tackle and also about how and why good dry-fly tackle differs from tackle meant for other forms of flyfishing.

To go into all those questions now would interrupt us. Both you and I, or so I suspect, would like to discuss trout and their habits just as soon as we can. Tackle, however important it may be, is less fascinating by far. Nor will the best tackle teach anyone how to catch trout. So let us hurry over the salient points, and leave the rest till later.

RODS

a) *Material*

Excellent dry-fly rods can be made either from carbon fibre or from built cane, and very, very serviceable ones can be made from fibreglass. The only small drawback glass rods have is that their 'action' (the way they cast) is often a little less smooth and doesn't reach right down 'into the hand'.

As against this, glass is very durable and lighter than cane. I have caught many fish on glass rods. Glass is also the least expensive of rod materials. The most expensive is carbon fibre, followed by cane.

Cane is the heaviest of rod materials and carbon fibre is the lightest. Cane is therefore best suited to short or average-length rods (8 feet 6 inches or under). A long cane rod can be tiring, so if you want a rod of, say, 9 feet, it's usually wise to choose glass or better still, carbon fibre.

All three materials have their supporters and detractors. But don't let anyone tell you that one material is a gift from Heaven while the other two are inventions of the devil. It just isn't true. All have their place and all can be made into good rods.

b) *Length*

Not so long ago nearly all dry-fly rods used to be 9 feet long or over. Better construction now means that rods powerful enough for almost any river—whether they be cane rods or glass rods—can be 9 feet or *under*. These modern rods are lighter and handier. It is possible to buy 'midge' rods of only 6 feet, which weigh only 2 ounces and can throw a long line. But such a rod is usually a little too short to be convenient. A good length for dry-fly fishing on a small brook is about 7 feet. Longer rods are needed for wider streams and the best all-round length is probably between 8 feet and 9 feet.

It is a handicap for any beginner—man or boy—to have too short a rod when he is first learning how to cast. One of his main difficulties will be managing to keep his back-cast high up in the air, and a short rod makes this even harder to do. A good rod for a beginner should be no less than 8½ feet and it can be 9 feet.

c) '*Action*'

It is very easy to be confused by the various phrases used to explain the 'actions' of different rods. Mostly it boils down to common-sense. A good dry-fly rod should not be so stiff and pole-like that it needs a very heavy line to bend it. Nor should it be so floppy that it has no backbone or 'punch'. Dry-fly fishing demands far more of a rod, and of the man wielding it, than does any other kind of flyfishing. If the rod is too 'fast' it will not be delicate. If it is too 'slow' it will not cast accurately into a wind. So the best dry-fly rod achieves a balance between all these factors. Perhaps the most useful word of advice is to say: 'Don't be led into thinking that the most *powerful* rod will necessarily be the best'. It is likely to be tiring to use, and rather clumsy. Do not seek more power than you need.

REELS

A reel should be large enough to accommodate the line that goes best with your rod, plus sufficient 'backing'. Backing is the thin line that comes after your casting line. It allows a large fish to run a long way and take out more than the mere thirty yards of casting line. A 3½ inch reel is an average size, but a 3¼ inch reel often suffices. It will always suffice if you use a forward-taper line, which takes up less room on a reel than the more common double-taper line.

A dry-fly reel, so long as it will hold the line, should be as small as is practicable—in aid of greater lightness. In the old days people used to talk a great deal about the reel 'balancing' the rod. When dry-fly rods were longer and more top-heavy, this was quite relevant—since a comparatively heavy reel could counter-balance the top-heaviness of a long rod. The concept is still relevant for long reservoir or loch-fishing rods. But light modern dry-fly rods, if they are to be as pleasant to use as they ought to be, deserve lightweight reels.

Nor need dry-fly reels be in the least complicated. Provided that they are well-engineered they can be very simple. It is possible to buy multiplying reels, reels with slipping clutches and reels with clockwork mechanisms for recovering line. All these have their uses, but seldom in dry-fly fishing. They involve extra cost and, more important, extra weight.

LINES

a) *Silk or Plastic*

The secret of modern 'floating' lines lies in their plastic dressing, which gives them a lower specific gravity than water. This means that they float without greasing—unless the plastic dressing becomes coated with scum or floating algae. Then they simply need to be wiped clean, and they will float again. Another advantage of them is that they have very 'sheer' surfaces which shoot easily through the rings of a rod for extra distance. And unlike silk lines they can be left on the reel to dry, without being in danger of perishing.

Silk lines, however, have their assets too. They are a little thinner for their weight than plastic floating lines (particularly at the tip) and so land a trifle more delicately on the water. They also offer rather less air-resistance when you are casting into a wind. If they are well-greased, they will float right along their length—while the last eighteen inches of a plastic line are hardly ever completely buoyant. And if care is taken to take them off the reel to dry after use, so that the air can get at them, they will last a long time.

So both silk and plastic lines have their respective advantages. But a beginner is perhaps well advised to start with a plastic line. It makes casting easier to learn, because it shoots so well through the rod-rings. And it invariably 'picks up' cleanly from the surface of the water. When casting has become a matter of habit, he can always change to a silk line if he finds he needs extra delicacy.

b) *Weight*

By far the most important aspect of a 'balanced' set of equipment is that the line should be of the right weight for the rod. If a line is too heavy, it can easily strain or break a rod. And even short of this, the rod will find it difficult to keep too heavy a line up in the air.

It is far more common, however, to see lines being used which are too light. Then the rod does not flex properly (it has to flex against the weight of the line) and fails to propel the line and fly as it should. The shorter the distance being cast, the worse the problem becomes, because a short length of line beyond the rod-tip is of course lighter than a long one. People may then think that there is something radically wrong with their casting, when with a heavy enough line they might cast perfectly well.

Line-weights are now specified by AFTM (Association of Fishing Tackle Manufacturers) numbers. The numbers range from 1 to 12 and are normally shown after the symbol #. Thus #1 designates the lightest flyline and #12 the heaviest. For trout-fishing a #3 line is as light a line as will ever be used. #5 is still a light line, for delicate fishing. #6 is an average weight. Any line over #7 will tend to be too heavy, and to land too splashily on the water, to be used for dry-fly fishing.

Nearly all rods made nowadays have an AFTM number stamped or inscribed on them, near the butt. This gives the weight of line which will best suit the rod when it is used by someone casting an average distance of a little over ten yards. The line you buy should never be lighter than this, or it will not bring out the rod's action. It can sometimes be heavier, if you are casting short distances only—but then be careful not to over-strain the rod.

c) *Double-taper or forward-taper*

On page 205 (in Appendix A) you will find a diagram which shows the different types of taper for a flyline. Level lines make good casting virtually impossible. The two types of line which can be used for dry-fly fishing are double-taper and forward-taper (or weight-forward), and each has something to be said for it.

If you look at the way in which double-taper and forward-taper lines are made up you will see that there is no visible difference in the front part—the first 30 feet. The big difference comes immediately after this. Whereas a double-taper line continues with a thick 'belly', a forward-taper line tails quickly off into thin 'running' or 'shooting' line.

Imagine yourself false-casting, and aerialising just the first thirty feet. If you then want to shoot quite a lot more line with your final cast, you can do so easily if you are using a forward-taper line—because the thin 'shooting' line goes out easily through the rod-rings and offers very little air-resistance. The thick belly of the double-taper line will not shoot nearly so well.

So far, so good. But if you want to *aerialise* more than thirty feet of line—as opposed to shooting it—you will have to use a double-taper line. If you try to aerialise more than thirty feet of a forward-taper line, the thick part gets too far away from the rod-tip and you lose control.

So a double-taper line is simpler to use—because you can aerialise as much or as little of it as you like. But if you shoot line, you will be able to cast further with a forward-taper line. You will also be able to cover fish more quickly, because it takes less time to shoot extra line than to aerialise it. This is a useful advantage when you have to cover a cruising fish in still water before he cruises out of range. And a forward-taper line casts a little better into a wind.

It is probably best to start with a double-taper line. (It has two usable ends, which is an economy.) But as you progress, you may well find that a forward-taper line will suit you better.

LEADERS (OR CASTS)

Everyone used to use the word 'cast' to describe this item. Many people still do. But it is very easy to muddle with the 'cast' that a fisherman makes when he is casting. So the word 'leader', which has been used for some time in America, is now gaining popularity here. I personally prefer it.

A good dry-fly leader should taper, of course, as does the line. And, which is more rare, it should carry on the taper of the line in as uninterrupted a way as possible—if it is to present the fly really well. Many ready-made leaders have butts which are a little on the thin side. Then there is too big a jump from the diameter of the line-tip to that of the leader-butt, especially in the case of plastic floating lines.

This is one reason why it pays to make up your own leaders, with different diameters of nylon joined together by blood-knots. The butt should be fairly long and should consist of pretty thick nylon (ideally 20 lb.). The tip should naturally be fine—2½ lb. for really fine fishing, or up to about 6 lb. for large trout or large flies. The lengths of nylon between butt and tip should 'step down' by easy stages.

A leader like this will give you the best chance of presenting a fly as you would like to, though some of the knotless tapered leaders available are almost as good. It is worth remembering that large bushy flies do not 'carry' well if they are attached to very fine nylon, since it may be too limp to overcome air-resistance. Equally, small flies will float unnaturally if attached to thick nylon.

NETS AND BAGS

A good net is essential, and I have already allowed myself to say a word or two in the first chapter about my pet hate in nets, the collapsible triangular sort. I must admit that they are convenient to pack and carry. But unless a fisherman has a lot of travelling to do, he will be better equipped with a net that has a rigid head. He will lose no precious time in getting the net unfolded, and furthermore he can probe for a fish in the weed with it.

It is not so necessary to be pernickety about a bag. Many people, indeed, use pockets or fishing waistcoats instead. Some use a straw fish-frail (sometimes called a fish-bass) to carry their fish in. But if you buy a bag, as most people do, a waterproof one is an advantage. It should be large enough to hold all you need. And let the strap be broad, or it will cut into your shoulder whenever the bag is weighed down by the results of a good day's fishing.

ACCESSORIES

There are a hundred and one accessories and impedimenta which a fisherman can carry with him. Some are valuable, while others are only of the barest theoretical use. Many are simply fun. Gadgetry is an exceptionally harmless form of fun, and no-one should try to deny us our gadgets. But the number of gadgets which any fisherman carries is strictly up to him.

If you use a silk line, you must have some line-grease. You may also find it useful for your leader and for the last eighteen inches or so of a plastic line, but in this case make sure, for the sake of preserving the dressing, that it is a non-silicone type of grease. Then some form of fly 'floatant', which you can get in either a bottle or an aerosol spray, can be helpful for anointing the fly so as to make it float better. And you will need a fly box to keep your flies in.

Some fishermen like to know what a trout has been feeding on, once they have caught him. This is always intriguing, and

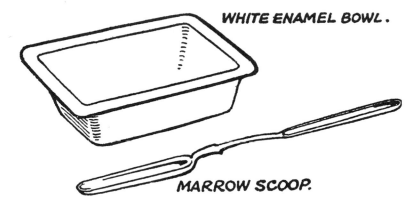

WHITE ENAMEL BOWL.

MARROW SCOOP.

sometimes it indicates which artificial fly will be the best at that moment. There are several ways of going about it. Often several of the flies which a trout has been taking will still be in his mouth or throat or gullet. A small but long-handled spoon helps to get them out. There are also pipette-like devices and the old 'marrow-scoops' (rather hard to come by) which will reach right into a trout's stomach. Or a complete autopsy can be performed and the trout's stomach can be slit open with a penknife. Then the contents can be dipped in a small glass or bowl, which should preferably be white, so that they separate and become distinguishable. You may well wish to keep the necessary instruments in your bag.

There is one other accessory which is invaluable. I never seem to have it when I need it most. I usually find, whenever I want to clear old nylon from the eye of a fly, that I have

forgotten to stick in my lapel that most useful of all inventions—
a pin.

FLIES

Thank goodness there is such a host of artificial flies. We may
only use a fraction of the number of patterns available, but life
would be far less fascinating if there were fewer of them. Some
of them are weird concoctions, and some are wild flights of
fancy—but they all have their own interest. I shall try to cover
the most effective patterns a little later on, when we discuss the
times of the season at which the different species of natural fly
usually hatch. But let us leave all these inanimate items of
tackle for the moment, and talk about trout.

PART TWO

TROUT, TROUT WATERS AND FLIES

Chapter 4

His Lordship

There is only one species of trout native to the British Isles, and his Latin name is *Salmo trutta*, a name which used to be reserved for sea trout alone. While you often hear about brown trout, gillaroo trout, slob trout, lake trout and so on, as well as sea trout, it is now definitely believed that all these are just different varieties of the same fish—*Salmo trutta*. The changes in colour, markings and size have been brought about by their varying environments.

The trout we most often fish for inland is commonly called a brown trout, and he spends his whole time in fresh water. The sea trout, on the other hand, is born in fresh water but travels down to the sea as soon as he is old enough to make the journey. Then he lives and grows in salt water and only comes back into fresh water to spawn. How two members of exactly the same species developed such contrary habits may always be a mystery. One possible theory is that the brown trout once lived in the sea. When the ice-packs retreated from Southern Europe, many of the trout found the seas too warm for them and sought refuge in the cooler waters of freshwater rivers, where some were afterwards landlocked in lakes. But it is just as likely that our present sea trout once lived in fresh water and migrated at some stage to richer feeding-grounds in the oceans.

Another sort of trout which you may catch is the rainbow trout (*Salmo gairdneri*). The rainbow is a different species altogether, and he is not a native of the British Isles but was originally imported in 1884 from the western seaboard of North America. He does not breed very well in this country, and there are only a few rivers here in which he has reproduced naturally and established himself. (The Derbyshire Wye and Buckinghamshire Chess are two of them.)

But to make up for this, he has turned out to be very useful

33

for 'stocking' purposes once he has been artificially reared. Although he only lives about half as long as a brown trout, he grows about twice as quickly. This means that he is rather cheaper to rear to a catchable size. Many reservoirs and other waters are now stocked with a high proportion of artificially-bred rainbows—and when you hook one you soon discover why they have earned such a high reputation as 'acrobats' on the end of a line.

This borrowing of the rainbow from America has by no means been a one-way affair. The Americans in their turn began importing the brown trout from Europe at the end of the last century, and they found that he had no trouble in reproducing naturally there.

Brown trout have also been taken to many other countries— as far apart as India and New Zealand—and have nearly always proved themselves first-rate, hardy colonists.

Trout, biologically speaking, are 'vertebrate animals', or 'backboned animals'—just as human beings are—but with fins

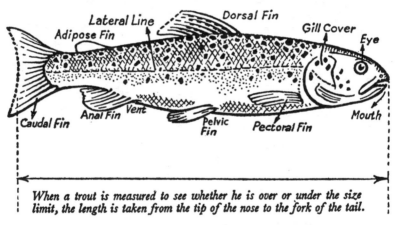

When a trout is measured to see whether he is over or under the size limit, the length is taken from the tip of the nose to the fork of the tail.

instead of limbs and able to breathe in water. They do this by taking in water through their mouths, then passing it out through their gills. Tiny blood-vessels in the gill filaments— those red flaps you will find inside their gill covers—extract some of the oxygen dissolved in the water and pass it into their bloodstream. This is why the trout you see in rivers always lie in the same direction, facing the current. If they faced down-stream in flowing water it would flow the wrong way through their breathing system and they would literally drown.

And this is also why, when dry-fly fishermen walk along a river bank looking for rising trout, they nearly always walk upstream. Then they can be reasonably certain of approaching a fish from behind with a much better chance of seeing him before he sees them.

Even at the best of times, however, trout are not particularly easy to see because they have a valuable gift for blending their colouring to match their backgrounds. They can change their colour and markings by the concentration or dispersal of light and dark pigments in their skin. Of course, they do not make quite such a good job of it as the chameleon, and they take a good deal longer about it—but still, this colour-blending is very useful. The pigments rearrange themselves according to the light rays reaching the trout's eyes from underwater objects. So blind trout often become black or dark in colour.

A trout's senses are tremendously important to fishermen, and the rest of this chapter will be spent in explaining them. The eyesight of a trout probably influences dry-fly fishing more than any of his other senses. A trout's eyes are on either side of his head. They do not always have to look to the front, as our

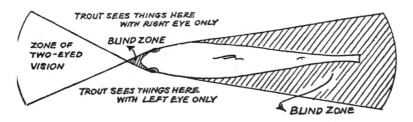

eyes do, so he has a much greater range of vision; but his eye-sight within this range is perhaps not so precise, since he can see most things with only one of his eyes and has very little two-eyed, or binocular vision—so vital to the judging of distance.

The scope of a trout's vision can be seen in the drawing above. Just behind his back he has a blind area—the advantages of approaching him from down-stream become even more obvious. To his left and his right there are large one-eyed or monocular areas, while in front he has a fairly limited two-eyed area where he can judge distance very well.

When you stalk a trout from the side he can only see you with one eye, so he finds it very difficult to tell exactly how far away you are. If you approach him in a straight line he will seldom be frightened because there seems to him to be little apparent change in the landscape. If you make a sideways movement, however, he can see it much more quickly and may be off in a flash.

Interestingly enough, fish like the trout, which not only catch but often have to pursue their prey, usually have their eyes set farther forward in their heads than other fish. In this way they sacrifice a certain amount of the view behind them so that they can gain a wider range of two-eyed vision in which to judge distance and hunt effectively.

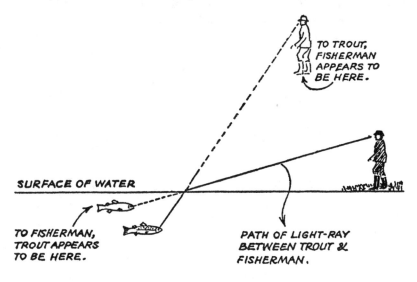

TO TROUT, FISHERMAN APPEARS TO BE HERE.

SURFACE OF WATER

TO FISHERMAN, TROUT APPEARS TO BE HERE.

PATH OF LIGHT-RAY BETWEEN TROUT & FISHERMAN.

A trout's sight of things above the water is largely governed by the refraction of light as it meets the surface. The eyesight of trout, like our own, depends upon the fact that the eye can pick up rays of light travelling towards it from anything within view. Now, all light rays entering the water from the air, or vice versa, are refracted. They are bent downwards. If you place a half-crown in a basin, put the basin on a table and then stand back a little from the table, the rim of the basin will eventually hide the half-crown. But if someone fills up the basin with water while you are standing there, a small miracle seems to occur. The half-crown again becomes visible. You are actually looking at a point just above the half-crown, but the refracted light rays allow you to see over the rim.

You can imagine this effect from the point of view of a trout just beneath the surface. The diagram shows it. Now imagine *all* the light rays coming to him in this way—remembering also that light striking the water from an angle of less than ten degrees is nearly all reflected *from* the surface. The result is as shown in the diagram below.

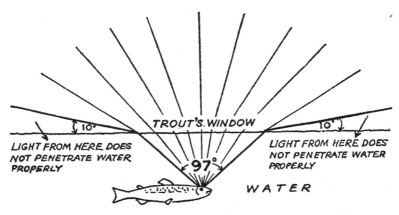

Everything a trout sees above the water is crowded into a small window in the surface, which is usually called the 'trout's window'. He can *only* see through his window. The light rays which hit the water outside his window do not come to his eye at all. The deeper the trout is in the water, the larger his window becomes and the more he can see.

So if you come upon a trout lying only just below the surface of the water you can take it for granted that he will notice a good deal less of what is happening above it than a trout rather further down. However, if a trout goes too deep down, particularly in cloudy water, he will not see you at all clearly

because the water itself absorbs light. Light rays cannot
penetrate very far into it without losing their strength.

Again whenever light strikes the surface of the water some of
it is always reflected back into the air. It never gets as far as the
trout's·eye—and the lower the starting point of the light, the
less of it actually goes into the water. This is why fishermen
always keep low on the river bank. If a ray of light comes to the
water from directly above, most of it passes into the water. Of a
ray meeting the surface at an angle of 45 degrees, about half
passes in. But at an angle of 10 degrees nearly all of it is reflected

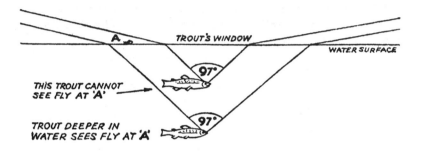

back into the air. A trout's view of things low on the bank is
therefore very indistinct indeed, so that it is easy to realise the
importance of keeping well down as you stalk a fish.

On either side of a trout's window he sees the surface as a
mirror. No light comes through to him from above, while all
of the rays coming from the stones and weeds beneath are
turned back by the surface itself. He sees only the river bed.
The top of the water acts as a complete ceiling of mirrors,
except for that one circular window directly above, through
which the trout gets a rather blurry view of air and land,
distorted by distance and the refraction of light, and perhaps by
ripples or eddies on the surface.

When you cast a floating fly to a trout it is well worth
remembering that he cannot notice anything outside his window
on the surface. So if you take care to let neither your line nor
the thicker part of your leader float into the window you are
less likely to frighten him than if they do. Unless your fly itself

does float into it, however, he will ignore your offering completely, simply because he cannot see it. Things below the water he can see clearly. He can see a sunk fly at a far greater distance than a floating fly because it is on the near side of his ceiling of mirrors. He will often, for instance, come quite a long way to take a sunk wet fly or nymph, far further than he would for a true dry fly.

When you come to choose flies yourself it is useful to know something about the trout's ability to distinguish between different colours and sizes. Fortunately, some recent research has filled in certain gaps in our knowledge. Some people say that trout are colour-blind. Therefore, they maintain, the colour of a fly doesn't matter. Scientists, however, have proved them wrong. Trout may not see the same spectrum as we do. They may see more colours, or fewer colours, but it's been shown that like most fish they can distinguish colour differences.

Some fish, for instance, if they are fed exclusively on a diet of blood-worms, can easily be taken in by bits of red wool, but not by blue wool, green wool or yellow wool. Again, if you feed them the whole time through blue eye-droppers, they will soon learn to swim to blue eye-droppers even if they are empty. They will not swim towards empty eye-droppers of any other colour. Many tests like this have indicated that fish do have a sense of colour—while other tests, using shades of grey, have shown that this seems to be quite separate from their sense of shade and brightness.

How about size? Most fishermen have known plenty of days when a change in the size of their fly has been more effective than a change in the pattern. Size can certainly be very important. And shape? Tame carp, again, have shown in tests that they can distinguish between triangles, circles and squares. But then carp, by nature, approach their food slowly and have a certain amount of time to look at it. Trout take their food at a fair speed, and in their case it is quite possible that the general appearance of a fly, as the light shines through it, or perhaps the motion given to it by the current or its own strugglings, is at least as important as its exact shape.

Certainly an old, well-chewed, battle-worn fly often seems just as tasty to trout as a brand-new one with not a feather out of place. It seems fair to say that although the general outline, colour and translucency of a fly—and the way it rides on the water—are noticed by the trout, they very seldom bother to examine the more tiny details of it.

Luckily, trout do not always seem to make full use of their powers of perception and judgement. Sometimes they seem so bemused by hunger or, for all we know, by spring fever or mid-summer madness, that they snap up nearly any apology for a fly. On these so-called duffers' days the school of any-fly's-as-good-as-the-next comes home happy. On days of a different sort, all the trout in the river seem gifted with an uncanny genius for telling artificial flies from the natural ones. Then the fly-maker's art really comes into its own. Good flies—flies tied skilfully from carefully selected materials—will always look more like the real thing than bad ones do, because they let through the right kind of light, because they dance on the water and because they somehow appear to be alive.

During the evening, as the light fades, you may find that you can get rather closer to your trout than you could in broad daylight. But since the trout has a special apparatus in his eye which enables him to see in dim light better than human beings can, it is as well not to overdo this. Only too often trout see us perfectly well when we never catch a glimpse of them. It might be a little disturbing to know how many feeding trout we frighten each time we walk up a river bank. Sometimes they leave bow-waves behind them as they dash away. More often, perhaps, they just sink very quietly down in the water, and leave us no indication of the opportunities we may have missed.

Trout may see less well when they look into the sun than when they look away from it. They cannot contract the pupil of their eye quickly, and may tend to be dazzled, whereas if they look in the other direction they can see objects on the surface clearly against the sky. So if you fish for trout with the sun behind you, you may have a slight advantage. But then take care to remember that a trout is always very frightened when the shadow of a fisherman falls across his window.

So much for the trout's vision. Now for his hearing. There is an old myth that fishing wives are never allowed to speak to their husbands because it might frighten the fish. So far as trout-fishing is concerned this is quite untrue. Most trout will seldom be scared even by a pistol-shot on the bank.

Trout can hear, however. All hearing consists of sensing vibrations, and a trout can certainly sense vibrations in the water, even if these start in the air. He has hidden ears of a sort, and he can also hear with his lateral line, the long line running down each side of his body. This is sensitive to vibrations, too. Stamping around on a river bank or banging about in a boat, therefore, is never a good idea, and if wading is necessary nothing can be lost by moving in the water as delicately as possible.

On the other hand, aeroplanes have been breaking the sound-barrier nearly every day recently just by the little stream I fish in Hampshire. Although the bangs have created a great uproar among the local cattle and pheasants, I cannot say that I have ever known a trout affected by them. If the trout happened to be feeding at the time, they continued to feed. That is only my own experience, however. It has been proved that some laboratory fish are very good at distinguishing different sounds, and therefore it is probably wise to play safe and avoid too much racket on the bank. Even so, it is extremely unlikely that trout will ever be frightened by a wife's conversation—or even by the habitual cursing of dry-fly fishermen when things go wrong.

Like some human beings, fish can develop certain senses at the expense of others. The trout hunts by eyesight so, quite naturally, his vision is better than his senses of taste and smell. Yet a trout has smell-buds in his nostrils. Biologically there is no reason why a trout should not have a sensitive sense of smell if he finds it useful. Nocturnal feeders such as dog-fish track down their food almost entirely by smell, and it is quite possible that large old trout, who often hunt by night, have also learned to smell fairly well. The majority of trout, however, probably do not smell their food before they eat it, particularly in fast water.

Trout have taste-buds, too, concentrated chiefly in their mouths but also scattered all over their skin. Though human beings can only taste in their mouths, many fish—the goldfish is one—can taste over their entire outer surfaces. It has been shown that fish are capable of distinguishing between sweet, salt, sour and bitter. (Without a sense of smell to help us, these are the only tastes we can distinguish ourselves.) Often and often a trout will pick out a particular sort of fly on the water when there are many larger flies hatching at the same time. There seems absolutely no reason why this should not be due to the fact that smell and taste combine to make some flies more palatable.

All fish have an acute sense of temperature; they can detect even small variations very quickly. Every fish has a normal range of temperature that lets him live comfortably. In the case of some fish this range includes high temperatures, and in the case of others fairly low ones, but in either case a fish can only stay alive within its own particular limits. It quickly dies if these are overstepped. Trout begin to be in danger when the water-temperature is in the seventies.

When trout farmers transfer young trout from cans to a river, they always spend some time bailing water slowly out of the cans and replacing it with river water so that any small change in temperature takes place gradually and does not distress the fish. Sudden changes of temperature, even within their temperature range, often harms them. In warm weather trout go to the cooler parts of a lake or river, only returning to the shallower parts with colder weather.

That is a brief résumé of the trout's physical senses. Perhaps it is worth mentioning that the experts consider it more or less impossible for fish to experience pain on anything like the same scale as we do. Here is a comforting thought for fishermen.

There is one further aspect. You will often hear trout described as artful, cunning and resourceful. This is far too flattering. No trout thinks. His behaviour is usually dictated purely by instinctive responses, although these may have been influenced a little by his own experiences. If he takes the dry fly you offer him he does so because this is his response to something that looks like food at a time when he is hungry. If he refuses it he does so because it does not look like the food he wants. Probably he is not even frightened. He may have learned from experience that unnatural-looking insects with fibres trailing from their noses are not particularly edible, but he certainly does not work out that anyone is trying to catch him. Similarly, when a trout breaks your cast in the weeds or round some sunken roots he does so only because he has found that his best response to any strange danger is to seek the nearest refuge. A trout's brain is very small. It is sometimes said that dry-fly fishermen 'pit their brains against those of the trout'. No-one has ever levelled a bigger insult at us.

Chapter 5

His Element

Trout always like living—and grow best—where there is plenty of food. Water in itself is a rather inhospitable element, because pure water, distilled water, contains no nourishment for any living plants or animals, let alone trout. Fortunately the water in lakes and rivers is not pure—it has collected from the ground certain substances called salts. These salts—which go by names like phosphate, sulphate and nitrate—are usually dissolved in the water, though sometimes they exist in particles of earth carried along by the current. If there are plenty of them the water is called rich, and if there are rather few it is usually described as poor. Salts are the earliest link in the food-chain and support the first living things, which are plants. Big plants and small plants alike live on the salts. The smallest plants are the algae—microscopic green or blue-green vegetables that either float around in still water, without roots at all, or moor themselves firmly to under-water objects. Incidentally, the film that covers most sunken stones and weeds consists of millions of these minute algae.

The algae are the food of many tiny animals, including insects—such as the larvae of the flies which trout feed on—and these in turn are eaten by larger and larger animals, till the trout is reached. This food-chain is even carried on outside the water, when water-creatures nourish land animals or birds. In the end the dead animals and plants sink to the bottom where, if they are not eaten by other animals which feed by scavenging, their bodies are attacked by bacteria. Bacteria break down their corpses into the original materials from which they were built up so that the materials are let loose again in the water and help to make it even richer.

Wherever the water is rich, thousands of creatures of different sorts and sizes will live in it. It becomes like a jungle in miniature. The richer the water, the more creatures there will be. All of them play a part in the food-chain. Nearly all of them, if they are not trout food themselves, are the food of the trout's food, or perhaps even the food of the trout food's food, and in the end they all rely on the dissolved salts in the water.

So rich water usually breeds the fattest trout, though poor water—provided other conditions are right—may provide a home for quite a number of small ones. In general, hard or alkaline waters are rich in nutrient salts and soft or acid waters rather short of them. Mountain streams that flow over hard rock or through barren soil have little chance to pick up valuable salts and are therefore usually acid. Hard, unfertile country produces soft waters which are usually also acid—like the small streams of Scotland and Cornwall. These waters may have plenty of trout in them, but the scarcity of food will prevent them growing very big. An alkaline stream of the same size, say in Hampshire, will be richer in food and more prolific as regards large trout. Both chalk and limestone districts can usually be counted upon for particularly good fishing waters—partly because rivers and lakes there have a very good supply of a substance called calcium, which always helps to enrich the water.

Oxygen is as essential to trout as food is. All underwater animals breathe oxygen, as land animals do, and a fish out of water dies not because there is less oxygen in the air— actually there is more—but because his special way of breathing is only suited to extracting oxygen from water. All water contains some oxygen; but since the animals are constantly using it up the supply needs continual replenishing. This can happen in various ways.

A little oxygen seeps very slowly through the surface from the air, and where the current is fast and the surface choppy the water mixing with the air hastens the process. Well-aerated water, like the water in a pool beneath a waterfall, is usually full of oxygen—and often full of trout. But the most useful means of all is through the action, once more, of plants.

All plants, during the day, go through the process of photo-synthesis. That is, they breathe in carbon dioxide from the water and use it for their own nourishment. Then they breathe out oxygen. Scientists know very little about how this process actually works except that a green pigment called chlorophyll plays a large part in it, but on a fine, sunny day you can often see the bubbles of oxygen coming up from underwater plants.

Thanks to photosynthesis, plants can contribute a great deal of the oxygen used by trout and other water animals; these, in return, breathe out the carbon dioxide used by plants. During the night, however, plants take in oxygen and give out carbon dioxide like animals, because photosynthesis can only take place under light. Even so, green plants nearly always produce, on balance, more oxygen than they absorb.

The store of oxygen in any stretch of trout water can be seriously endangered by several causes. The warmer water gets, the less oxygen it can hold. And decomposing matter, like dead leaves, animal corpses, or sewage, takes up oxygen very quickly. Deoxygenation is often caused by pollution, always a very real threat to country-lovers, whoever they may be.

Pollution takes two common forms, the worst of which is the dumping in the river of sewage or other decomposing waste matter. Decomposition on such a large scale can easily rob the water completely of oxygen. The other, less usual type of pollution, is neither more nor less than direct poisoning, when a factory discharges chemicals that kill trout. Both sorts of pollution can be lethal, but happily the laws of the country, plus the work of the Angler's Co-operative Association and other bodies, do give a measure of protection against pollution. Even so, we can never have too much protection—if we want our grandchildren to be able to fish, or even to paddle safely.

There are, however, other dangers. As an example, imagine a small pond, full of vegetation, on a still, warmish autumn day. Dead leaves have fallen into it and are absorbing oxygen. Perhaps, to make matters worse, some unlucky animal has drowned in the pond and is using up even more oxygen while bacteria decompose its carcase. Despite all this, the waterplants have produced enough oxygen during daylight to sustain life in the pond.

When night comes—particularly if it is a warm night— the situation may change for the worse. Suddenly the plants, instead of producing oxygen, are competing for it themselves.

In a few hours the pond may become uninhabitable, but there is no escape for the animals in it and by the time morning arrives many of them may be dead. Here is one of Nature's often-unnoticed tragedies. If you own a goldfish pond in your garden you should take care to clean the dead leaves out of it when autumn comes. The goldfish, however, has one peculiar characteristic—he needs less oxygen than any other fish. That is why you can keep him in a bowl with no plants growing. Trout, on the other hand, like more oxygen than many fish and always thrive in the best oxygenated places.

The oxygen content of larger ponds, and of lakes, seldom goes through such wild fluctuations. On a wide open sheet of water the wind helps to mix the water with the air. In a river the current achieves the same end, and the flowing water helps to keep the temperature fairly constant.

Food and oxygen are the two most important things in life to a trout. And because of this, food chains and oxygen chains are vitally important to trout water. It is well worth understanding how they both operate. A very simple example, on a small scale, can be seen in any ordinary water-butt filled with rainwater.

Rainwater is fairly pure, and therefore poor in salts, but it collects just enough of them on its journey through the air to support small colonies of algae. After the water has been standing for a little, a greenish film will start appearing on the sides of the butt. This is made by algae, beginning to establish themselves in a new-found home. Shortly afterwards some tiny animals will arrive to feed on the tiny plants. You will have to look very carefully to see them with the naked eye, but a fine muslin net drawn through the water will collect thousands of them. These are the pioneers of the animals. Sometimes they do quite well, build a highly successful empire and may attract some larger animals. But all too often they are much too greedy for their own good. They attack the algae and reduce them to the point where they can no longer release enough oxygen for the little world of the water-butt. The world dies. The whole cycle has to start all over again.

On a larger scale, exactly the same principles are at work in any trout-stream or any lake. It is easy to see how useful water plants are. The smallest of them—the algae—provide food for the smallest animals, and without small animals there will be no big ones.   The bigger plants are themselves covered with algae, and all the plants help to oxygenate the water. Also, of course, they give shelter to trout and trout-food.

Most of the water plants that grow to any size are called weeds, but whereas 'weeds' are ruthlessly eliminated in a garden, a good growth of weeds in a river is something to encourage. They only become a nuisance when they're the wrong kind or when extra-rich water makes them grow too thickly. Where they are too profuse they may cause a danger of flooding or stagnation, or collect too much mud round their roots, or leave too little open space for fishing. At this stage they have to be cut back.

Any water can be 'farmed'. Just as a farmer prefers fertile soil, a fisherman prefers fertile water; rich in nourishment for trout. As a farmer grows useful plants and gets rid of others, a fisherman can encourage the weeds that provide the best food and shelter for trout and do away with the rest. If the current is too fast for plants to root themselves properly, he can always slow it up by erecting little dams and groynes. If, on the other hand, the current is so slow that mud is deposited on the bottom, killing the weeds, he can make it faster, and clean the river-bed, by concentrating the flow between hurdles, or in some other way. Then he can improve his stock of trout by increasing their supply of natural food, even to the extent of protecting or rearing the animals that they eat. Wherever there is plenty of food and oxygen, and a fairly even, cool water temperature too, trout will live and breed and thrive.

Chapter 6

His Life

A. FOOD AND ENEMIES

Some weeks before Spring, young trout hatch from their eggs. They are funny-looking creatures, these freshly-hatched 'alevins'—about half-an-inch long, with round, monstrous eyes and huge bag-like affairs slung underneath their bellies. The bags are actually yolk-sacs, full of nourishment, which the trout gradually absorb during their first three or four weeks after hatching. At this time they seldom feed through their mouths at all, they have no scales, they are smaller than sticklebacks, and they may easily fall a prey to eels, fish, dragonfly nymphs or any creature larger than themselves. There are a great many of these larger creatures, so it is hardly surprising that only one alevin out of hundreds ever becomes an adult trout.

The little alevins hide themselves in the stones or gravel among which they hatched from the egg. For about three weeks they live in the 'redds'—as the places where trout lay their eggs are called—and subsist on their yolk-sacs. Towards the end of this time they begin making sorties into the stream, learning how to face the current and recognise food when they see it.

As his yolk-sac disappears an alevin starts to resemble a miniature trout. He is now a 'fry', with well-developed fins and pigmented skin. Soon the 'platelets' of the scales will appear. The fry takes up a position in the current and feeds on the small morsels which it brings him—morsels such as fly-larvae and young shrimps.

At this stage the difference between large and small trout first begins to show. A trout's rate of growth as compared with his fellows depends entirely upon the force and energy with which he hunts. Competition among trout-fry is ruthless, and the strongest and hungriest fry will always get the best food, shouldering the others out of the way. These bullies will grow best. Quite a few of the weaker fry will starve, while many others will only grow very slowly.

All trout, including trout-fry, are carnivorous and support themselves by eating any other members of the animal kingdom they can find. Often young trout eat much the same type of food as their elders do. But whereas mature trout prefer mature flies, larvae, shrimps and snails, the young fish batten upon the baby ones. In lakes, or in the very quiet parts of a river, trout-fry feed also upon zoo-plankton. These are microscopic animals which either float or swim around in the water. Water-fleas are among the most important of them and they make excellent food for young fry. There are less zoo-plankton in rivers than in lakes because a current soon washes them away.

As soon as the alevins turn into fry, they start fighting for good lies in the water. As they grow older they take over better and better lies. Trout have no love for each other, and except during the spawning season, when they pair, they lead a selfish, solitary existence. They do not welcome companions gladly. A trout's home may consist of no more than a slight hollow in the river-bed, but even so he will quickly chase other fish out of it if possible. When trout go house-hunting they look for three things—good cover, easy lying and plenty of food. The first of these can be provided by rocks or by tree-roots, or by holes in the bank or by weeds. Easy lying often goes with good cover. A trout never likes to swim hard all day merely to keep himself in a static position against a strong current. Therefore he chooses places out of the direct flow, in weed-beds, behind stones or perhaps where the bottom dips a little so that the main force of the current passes overhead. In lakes the consideration of easy lying does not count nearly so much. But in both lakes and rivers there still remains the question of food supply. A trout in a river would far rather have his food brought to him by the stream than go searching for it. After all, the current does provide an excellent meal service twenty-four hours a day. So your trout, although he prefers living out of the current, will often choose a home fairly near it so that he can make a swift sortie from behind his stone to seize any animal that is being swept down, or else take up a station beside his weed-bed to be within easy reach of floating flies when they are hatching on the surface.

In still water the trout also live close to their food. This means that they will usually avoid the very deepest water, for the sun's light cannot reach down there and trout food will be pretty sparse. On the other hand very shallow water is too exposed for them. They will live mostly between the shallows and the deeps, hovering near the weed-beds, roaming the open water in search of zoo-plankton, or hunting the animals that live in clean gravel or shingle. If the level of the water in a lake changes, or if its flow in a river alters, the trout will frequently look for new homes to suit the new conditions.

At the end of a year a trout becomes a yearling—no longer a fry. He is now an active little fish of four or five inches in length. He is sometimes called a fingerling. After two years, in a good chalk-stream, he is eight or nine inches long and it no longer takes a second look to pick him out from among the minnows. In the Spring of the next year he should be catchable —that is, twelve or thirteen inches long in a chalk-stream, and nearly a pound in weight. A rainbow trout takes only two years to reach the same weight as a brown trout does in three, which makes him a far cheaper proposition for trout-farmers to rear.

The growth of trout is a good deal slower in streams less rich in food than the Test and Itchen and other chalk-streams. In many West Country, Welsh, Irish and Scottish streams, a trout becomes catchable when he is only a quarter of a pound and six or seven inches long. It will still, however, have taken him about three years to grow up if he is a brown trout. Generally speaking, in any stretch of water there is enough food to maintain x pounds' weight of trout. The nature of the food will often decide whether you have, say, ten two-pound trout or twenty one-pound trout or forty half-pound trout. Flies, if there are plenty of them, are quite good trout-food, but very few trout exist on flies alone. If, for instance, they can get freshwater shrimps and snails as well, they seem to find these particularly nourishing and will grow large quickly. Other food like small insect-larvae and zoo-plankton will support a number of small fish but will hardly ever raise them to any great size.

There may, of course, be other types of fish in the water competing with the trout for the available food. Coarse fish of nearly any sort will eat bottom-food that might have served to nourish trout. In clear, fast, well-oxygenated water the trout have an advantage over the coarse fish and breed faster than the coarse fish, but in other types of water the coarse fish, once introduced, establish themselves fairly quickly and may even start evicting the trout. Grayling and salmon-fry, as well as coarse fish, deplete the supplies of trout-food. Both of them rely on much the same diet as trout, and the more there are of them in the river, the more competition there will be for the food—a struggle in which many trout may come off badly.

Added to competitors are predators. A trout spends his whole life in perpetual danger of losing it through attack from either the water or the air. He has several enemies in his own element, the most unpleasant of which is the pike. A pike can eat his own weight of trout very quickly if he is hungry.

Small trout are also very acceptable morsels so far as large trout are concerned. Trout of any size will catch and eat smaller fish whenever they can. Medium-size trout will pursue minnows, bullheads and trout-fry. So will larger trout—but they often snatch up yearling trout as well. As a trout grows bigger and stronger he is likely to prey more and more on other fish, since smaller mouthfuls of food are no longer enough to keep up his weight.

Then there are otters. A great deal of discussion has taken place as to whether these animals do great harm to trout water or not. The otter's defenders maintain that he really does little harm because he prefers eels to anything else. And they also argue that otters help to maintain a high standard of health among the trout by weeding out diseased and sickly fish. All this may sometimes be true. It may always be true. The trouble is that it is very difficult to prove. Once a water-bailiff has seen a few of his beloved trout lying dead on the bank, with bites in their shoulders to point out the guilt of otters, you will find it hard to convince him that co-existence between otters and trout is a very practical idea.

Birds, however, can be even worse enemies. The heron, particularly, is a skilful and dangerous fisherman. He has one great stock-in-trade—immobility. For hours a heron will stand motionless in shallow water till a trout ventures near him, perhaps searching for food, perhaps returning to a spot he left in fright when the heron first arrived. Then a quick, deadly flash of the beak, which he can wield just like a dagger, and it is all over. Gulls and even kingfishers also eat trout. Some wild birds—like these—may only be legally shot if 'serious damage' to a fishery can be definitely proved. Others may be shot anyway, others never. A kingfisher's beauty, law apart, makes him inviolate. Few people could loose off a charge of shot at that colourful, gleaming little bird, whose presence is so often the delight of a day's fishing, even though early in the morning, when there are few witnesses about, he and his family take a few trout-fry.

Cormorants and shags take their toll of trout, too. So also do poaching cats. A friend of mine once owned a house near a trout farm to which a neighbouring cat had attached herself. This tabby showed a really remarkable capacity for intelligent reasoning. Every day the trout-fry in the ponds used to be fed at regular hours and they had found out that whenever food was thrown into the water it created a disturbance on the surface. They came to recognise this disturbance as a summons to their meals. Even a handful of earth thrown in would make them gather round hopefully.

The cat used to watch the feeding of the trout frequently, with an apparently dispassionate air. But one day, as my friend looked out of his bedroom window at sunrise, he saw her approaching one of the ponds. Delicately, she went up to the edge and patted the water with her paw, making a series of little splashes. Immediately the young trout gathered round waiting like Lewis Carroll's oysters to be fed, whereupon all she had to do was to scoop one out and retire into the bushes for breakfast.

Trout undoubtedly have a very long list of enemies against

most of which only their speed of escape gives them any protection at all. It is therefore not in the least unnatural that they should be shy, nor that they should learn to be shy early. Trout-fry learn their lessons young and learn them quickly. Any shadow falling across the top of the water soon comes to be associated with a diving bird, while any unfamiliar shape moving along the bank can mean nothing but danger to them. But they also learn how to distinguish harmless animals from dangerous ones. If there are many cows in the meadows by the stream the trout will soon become quite accustomed to them, and they will also find out that they can live on friendly terms with ducks, coots and swans. Swans have an infuriating habit of swimming over rising trout just as you are beginning to fish for them. But the trout will not really be frightened if they know the swans well, or at any rate not for more than a minute or two. Soon they will be rising as eagerly as ever. Trout will sometimes feed practically under the necks of cows drinking in the river.

If the young trout survive, they go on adding to their weight year by year. The largest British trout known is the great Loch Awe fish, which weighed thirty-nine and a half pounds. He was caught in 1866 and then set up in a glass case. This was unfortunately destroyed by fire. Several other trout of over twenty pounds have been reliably reported, though the official record—as recognised by the British Record (Rod-caught) Fish Committee established in 1957—stands at a mere eighteen pounds and two ounces. This trout was caught in 1965, also in Scotland. But a great many trout in double figures have come from the big Irish lakes as well.

It may be surprising, but gigantic fish like these belong to exactly the same species as the little quarter-pounders we pull out of hill-streams. And they may not even be much older. They have simply fed better. They probably hatched in the little streams running into the big lakes, and grew there quite normally for some time, until one day they made their way down to the open water. There they found bigger and better food—such as the fry of other fish—and outstripped their brothers and sisters by twenty or thirty times.

By contrast, a trout is reputed to have lived in the bottom

of a well for fifteen years. At the end of this time the trout was
no heavier than a pound and a half, because there was not
enough rich food. This was one example of how food is more
important to the size of trout than age or heredity or any other
single factor.

Rainbow trout in this country do not grow to such a large
size as brown trout—mainly because of their shorter life-span.
They grow twice as quickly, but since they die at the end of
their fourth year they have no time to reach such massive
proportions. An eight-pound rainbow is not uncommon, but
the record is only just over ten pounds.

Although brown trout live longer, most of them begin to
go into a decline after six or seven years. For another year or
two they may maintain their weight but each Spring they
find it more and more difficult to get back into condition
after spawning. Then they probably lose weight, though they
may still add an inch or two to their length. Their heads
become large and ugly, their bodies lanky, their fins tattered,
their skin discoloured. Their increasing weakness makes them
worse and worse at hunting, and often blindness sets in as
well, first in one eye, then in both.

You sometimes see these pathetic victims of old age in the
streams, quite unaware of your approach, groping blindly
among the weeds for food, hoping perhaps to smell it where
they can no longer find it by sight. The best thing you can do
for them is to shoot them or wire them or lift them out with a
landing net.

Spawning always interrupts the growth of trout. They feed
very little while they are occupied in breeding, so that it
always takes them some time afterwards to replace the weight
they have lost. On the whole, female trout tend to reach
sexual maturity a year or two later than male trout and often
grow larger in the end because of this fact. Male trout in
hatcheries often spawn at the age of two. In natural conditions
they may start at the same age—or they may wait till they are
three or older. Once trout have spawned they usually spawn
again in each successive year. Round about the end of September
or beginning of October they move up towards the spawning-
beds, which are always clean, well-oxygenated, gravelly

shallows. This will probably be a pretty short journey if the
river is well supplied with good spawning grounds, but if it is
not the trout may travel a mile or more to find the right places.
Once they have arrived there, they wait in the shallows for a
week or two before they begin the actual process of spawning
in late autumn or winter.

Before the female trout spawn, they excavate little 'nests'
in the redds. They do this by performing violent bending and
arching body-movements over the gravel. Although this is
called 'cutting' they do not shift the gravel by physical contact
with it, but by the currents of water which their body-movements create. Meanwhile the males are usually engaged in
chasing each other or fighting among themselves—until one
of them is attracted by the cutting activities of a female. Then
he joins her and drives off other males.

When the nest is two or three inches deep, the female sheds
her eggs in it and the male fertilises them with his milt, almost
simultaneously. Immediately afterwards, the female moves just
upstream and covers the eggs with gravel by beginning to cut
her next nest. Each redd will consist of several nests and the
trout, resting occasionally, may take several days to complete
spawning. When it is over they drop slowly down-stream and
leave the eggs to take care of themselves.

The time of year for spawning varies considerably from
river to river. In some hill-streams the trout spawn in October,
while in the chalk-streams spawning trout have been seen as
late as February. The temperature of the water may influence
trout here. Trout eggs hatch in thirty-eight days at a temperature of fifty-two degrees Fahrenheit but they take a hundred
days at a temperature only ten degrees lower. The trout of
hill-streams may have learned to compensate for colder water
by spawning a little earlier.

The fate of the eggs is often rather a sad one—for many
of them come to grief. Trout lay about eight hundred eggs for
every pound of their weight. Some will be unfertilised. Others
may be choked by silt. The trout inside an egg needs oxygen
and the skin of the egg allows oxygen to pass through, but
not if silt is deposited on top. Other eggs, again, may be eaten
by water-animals, so that the mortality at this stage is huge,

practically impossible to estimate. A trout's chances of staying alive become increasingly better as he grows older; but just two trout eggs in a thousand, at a very optimistic guess, produce mature trout.

When trout have finished spawning they soon begin feeding again to get back their weight and strength. The early spawners and the smaller fish regain their condition soonest, provided that there is an abundant food supply. In some waters they are in fine fettle again by March, ready for an early start to the fishing season. But in Hampshire, because the trout are never really in fighting condition until April and sometimes not till May, the first day of the trout season has to be postponed till then. It is always a shame to take out thin, half-hearted fish before they can put up such a good resistance or make such a good meal as they might. The heavier fish always take longer to recover, as they have more bulk to build up.

Once they have started, trout go on feeding all summer, all autumn and even into winter. They are less hungry in the hottest months of the year than they were in the Spring, but in September and October they sometimes feed greedily again, perhaps to prepare for the lean time of spawning. There is a widespread idea that trout are rather pernickety about their fare. In reality, however, they will eat almost anything. Within the bounds of being carnivorous, trout are virtually omnivorous and they have been caught on unlikely things like mice. The same trout's stomach, when you have caught him on a Mayfly, may also contain beetles, tadpoles, worms, minnows, shrimps, snails and enough little animals of other sorts to start a small zoo.

All these will have been eaten during the last nineteen hours or so, which is roughly the time it takes a trout's digestion to work. The reason why he is often so very difficult to catch is that at any one particular moment he may be devoting himself exclusively to only one sort of food. You can seldom catch a trout rising to flies on a minnow, or a shrimping trout on a fly. The trout's willingness to come up to the surface for flies—and this obviously includes the fisherman's dry fly—depends on whether he is accustomed to feeding on flies, and on whether any of those flies are actually hatching at the time.

B. DRY-FLY WATER

Different types of lake, reservoir or stream produce different qualities of dry-fly fishing. Rivers, to start with, fall broadly speaking into four categories—sluggish, gentle, fastish and very fast—and each category has its own structure of animal life to influence the trout's behaviour.

First, sluggish rivers. These are the ones that flow so slowly that silt has been deposited on their beds in a thick carpet. Weeds find it easy to grow and there will be plenty of algae in the weeds. On the other hand the slowness of the water does not make for good oxygenation and the weeds take up a large amount of oxygen by night. Trout will not live here in very great numbers, nor will many of the flies most important to a dry-fly fisherman. March Browns, Dark and Medium Olives, and Iron Blues, to mention only four, all need plenty of oxygen passing over their bodies to allow them to breathe.

Most of the food in sluggish rivers, therefore, will consist of snails, beetles, worms and other animals only found well underneath the water. There will be a good many coarse fish to feed on them, and such trout as there are will feed on them, too. Or, if they are big enough, they may feed on the smaller coarse fish as Thames trout do. Fly-life will be fairly limited—and will be made up mainly of Mayflies, midges and some caddis-flies. You may have some sport, and even catch very lage fish when these flies put in an appearance, but on the whole there are not many trout in sluggish rivers and they are not regular surface-feeders.

Next, there are rivers that flow gently but not sluggishly, depositing silt only in certain places, and where the current is fast enough to keep areas of gravel or chalk bright and clean. These rivers, particularly if the water contains plenty of dissolved salts, may be the best of all. Good weeds—to provide cover and food for fly-larvae—will grow in both the gravel and the silt and there should be ample oxygen for both trout and insects. Invading coarse fish will not like it as much as the slower rivers and most river-flies will flourish there, showing themselves in a daily hatch sufficient to bring the trout up to the surface. As well as flies, you will find shrimps, snails, worms and all sorts of other nourishment for trout. There may even be crayfish. Crayfish need alkaline water and oxygen, and wherever they thrive the trout seem to grow big quickly. A fish has to reach a weight of about a pound and a quarter before he takes any real interest in these crustaceans—the largest in fresh water —but when he begins feeding on them he may even double his weight in a single year. So these gentle streams sometimes provide excellent dry-fly fishing, with plenty of large trout, most of whom may be frequent surface-feeders.

Then there are the slightly faster streams. If they flow fairly quickly over gravel but still have quite a few protected places where weeds can get a foothold, your fishing should still be good. As the stream runs faster and faster, and weed-beds thin out, you will find fewer and fewer Mayflies, Olives and Iron Blues, but their scarcity is often offset by rather more Stone-flies, March Browns and other flies. There will be a fair number of the caddis-flies who live in gravel, but not many shrimps or snails outside the few weed-beds. Trout food will become generally less plentiful as the weed-beds disappear, but even where the stream hastens and bubbles over rocks, moss can grow precariously on the stones and boulders to afford cover for insects, so that much of the available food continues to consist of flies, rather than of bottom-food. Oxygen is no problem. So on the faster streams, provided they are clear, you will nearly always find a trout *prepared* to feed on the surface. The trout here will be smaller on the whole, and you will not see many big hatches of fly such as the chalk-streams usually have every day. You may see very few rises or even none at all. But, perhaps for this very reason, the trout seem more continuously hungry and if you know where to find them, you can often bring them up by throwing a dry fly over them.

When the stream is so swift that it nearly always creates a turbulence on the top of the water, it is likely to be better for the wet fly than for the dry fly. There is no point whatsoever in sticking religiously to the dry fly when a sunk fly is more successful. Even on these streams, however, a dry fly can be more profitable than a wet fly at certain times, especially in high summer when the water is low and very clear. Apart from stagnant or polluted rivers, where there is no oxygen, the only ones that will support hardly any trout are those with beds of sand. A trout would have an exceedingly lean time of it there, because although weeds can consolidate themselves in silt and gravel, and moss or algae can cling to stones and boulders, shifting sand offers absolutely no anchorage for plants. And where there are no plants, there are seldom any small animals and insects for trout to eat.

Before leaving the rivers, it is worth noticing that there is an important difference between rain-fed and spring-fed streams. Those that are rain-fed, where the surface water from the ground runs directly into the river, are always subject to floods or spates. During a spate, fish and other large animals can take refuge from the pace of the torrent behind stones or in the quieter backwaters, but small animals like insects are often swept away and die. Droughts are another trouble, since insect-eggs and larvae may again be destroyed through being left high and dry by the falling water. Spring-fed streams—such as you find in many chalk districts—do not suffer from the same trouble. Here, the rain seldom rushes straight downhill to swell the river, but filters gradually through the chalk, reappearing in the springs weeks or even months later. The chalk acts, in fact, as a sort of reservoir, keeping the level of the water steady, guarding against spates and droughts equally. The trout-food is usually safer as a result, and one further advantage, from the fisherman's point of view, is that the river is all the less likely to get high and coloured. A tropical shower may make life unpleasant for him, but unless it lasts a long time it will not make fishing impossible by sending the river down looking like cocoa.

Finally, still water. The main difference between still water and flowing water, as regards trout-food, is the presence of zooplankton in still water. Zooplankton consists of minute free-floating organisms which live in lakes and reservoirs—otherwise they are carried away by the current—and most trout except the largest feed on them at times. They are very tiny creatures and seldom build big trout, although the whalebone whale—the largest animal that the Earth has ever known—does keep up his terrific bulk on their salt-water relatives. Trout in certain

Swiss lakes reach a weight of two pounds, feeding on nothing
but plankton.

Reservoirs and lakes often contain a large proportion of
bottom food and mid-water food. Some of it—such as shrimp
and coarse-fish fry—will go to nourish big trout. Sticklebacks
(which can be imitated by certain wet 'flies' and lures like the
Polystickle) are also eaten in quantity. The balance of the
trout's food, therefore, tends to weigh rather heavily against the
fish being likely to rise very frequently. The wet fly is usually a
better bet than the dry fly. But on some natural lakes, notably
the great lakes of Ireland, there are excellent hatches of Mayfly.
And on most reservoirs and lakes Sedges (or Caddis flies) and
midges will hatch in the evening. Nor is that the end if it.
Many still waters contain other flies as well—such as the Pond
Olive. Shallow lakes are on the whole better for still-water flies
than deep ones, because the larvae cannot live and grow where
the light never penetrates. A number of still-water flies prefer
rich, alkaline water, which rather limits their distribution, but
wherever they abound there may be good hatches of fly to
induce the trout to feed on the surface—at times. Then the dry
fly works.

To sum up, good dry-fly water can best be described as a
river, reservoir or lake where the trout come up to the surface
nearly every day to feed on hatches of fly. On any other water,
the best fisherman is the one who suits his method to the
weather, the time of the year and the behaviour of the trout on
the day he goes fishing. The wet-fly fisherman has every right to
look down his nose at a hide-bound dry-fly fisherman who waits
all day for a fish to rise where there are no flies to hatch, or
who fishes his fly on the surface of the water when the trout are
feeding well beneath it. The worm fisherman, too, can afford to
laugh at a man dry-fly fishing in a spate, because then the trout
will be gorging themselves on worms and grubs washed down
by the high water. The dry fly has its time and place on many
rivers and still waters—not all—and dry-fly fishermen use it
there, not because it makes them feel superior to wet-fly fishermen, but simply because it is more successful.

Chapter 7
Natural Flies

Is it really necessary for a fisherman to be able to tell which species of fly is hatching? Must he also imitate it exactly? Some fishermen—who have been dubbed purists —say that he must. But others go so far as to say 'any fly's the same as the next to a trout'. Another school, which believes in good casting, will tell you: 'It's not the fly, but the driver'. And there are still other fishermen who believe in steady, persistent fishing and say: 'The only successful fly is the one that's always on the water'. How very confusing! The truth is—of course—that everyone is perfectly right. Any fly will catch fish—at some times, and in some places. Good casting is a tremendous help at any time, and in any place. Persistent fishermen often catch trout when more skilful ones have packed up in despair. And, to give the purists their due, trout can sometimes be very choosy indeed.

The choosiest trout of all probably live in the chalk-streams. Occasionally they will only accept one sort of fly. But even on less heavily fished waters a fisherman who is also a bit of an amateur entomologist usually stands a better chance, even if it is sometimes only a slightly better chance, of catching trout than if he knew nothing at all about flies. And he has one further asset, which the purists sometimes do not admit to. He gets more sheer fun. Identifying living creatures is a fascinating hobby in its own right. Ask any bird-watcher. Fishermen must be rather like bird-watchers in this way.

Entomologists often call insects by their Latin names. This is not nearly so silly as it sounds. The trouble with the English names of flies is that there are so many of them for each sort of fly. For instance it would be quite possible for four fishermen to have an argument at the end of the day as to whether the flies on the water had been Dark Olives or Blue Duns or Spring Olives or Whirling Duns, and none of them might realize that they were all talking of the same fly. The Latin name for it is *Baëtis rhodani* and this is the only Latin name for it wherever it hatches, in any country. Latin names do avoid mixing flies up.

So I shall make no apology for mentioning the proper Latin names here. They may help to serve as a reference, even if you do not remember them. The flies which are most important to fishermen, because they are the most common as trout-food, can be divided into four main types—or 'orders', to use the right scientific word. Let me now sketch very briefly the characteristics and life-histories of these four 'orders'. Later on, in other chapters, I shall try to describe some of the individual flies more closely.

EPHEMEROPTERAN DUN
(WINGS UPRIGHT)

Here are the names of the four orders. First, the *Ephemeroptera* —or up-winged flies. Second, the *Trichoptera*—or sedge-flies. (These are sometimes also described as caddis-flies.) Third, the *Plecoptera* or stone-flies. And last, the *Diptera*—which include Gnats, Midges, Smuts and ordinary Bluebottles. There are a great many different flies within these four types, some of them common and some of them rare.

Most fishermen rely on the *Ephemeroptera* for the bulk of their sport. Mayflies, Olives and Iron Blues are all *Ephemeroptera* and when they hatch out they all have four wings which point up towards the sky like the sail of a boat. The front pair of wings is very large, usually slightly longer than the body of the fly itself, while the second pair is much smaller and very difficult to see since it is almost hidden by the first pair. No other flies carry their wings in an upright fashion and it is lucky that the

Ephemeropterans do. Their high wings make them much easier to spot on the water than any other sort of fly.

All the Ephemeropterans pass through four separate stages of development. Although they are called flies they can only fly for a very short period at the end of their lives. They start off as eggs, below the surface of the water. After a little time, which is usually a few weeks, these small eggs hatch out into nymphs— little grub-like creatures which still get their oxygen from the water and not from the air. The nymphal stage is by far the longest in the fly's existence. Most of them spend six months to one year as nymphs and Mayflies may even live in this form for two whole years.

If you buy a cheap muslin net at the village store, the sort of net that small children use for catching minnows, and then work it around in the weeds of a chalk-stream, it will come up with plenty of wriggling nymphs in it. On them depends the future sport that the stream will offer. They will vary in size and colour, since they will be the nymphs of various different flies at various ages. All of them, however, will represent those particular flies that like living in the weeds in running water. Not all nymphs do, and their separate preferences mean that you find different sorts of fly in different sorts of water.

Here are some of the preferences. All *Baëtis* nymphs like living in rivers and streams rather than in lakes. The genus *Baëtis* is a very large one within the *Ephemeroptera*, including the Dark Olive, the Medium Olive, the Iron Blue and two Pale Wateries. The nymphs of these flies, like many river-bred species, need water flowing past their bodies before they can absorb oxygen through their body walls. That is why the nymphs in the muslin net will very soon die if they are kept in a jam-jar. It is not so much the fact that there is too little oxygen in the jam-jar, but that the nymphs cannot make use of it unless the water is actually moving.

These nymphs are swimming nymphs. They are streamlined in shape, can dart quickly for a short distance and can make their way from weed to weed or stone to stone. Most of them can exist in either acid or alkaline water, though some occur rather more commonly in alkaline rivers such as the chalk-streams. Apart from the *Baëtis* flies there are one or two other swimming nymphs that exist only in rivers and there is one common still-water swimming nymph, the nymph of the Pond Olive (*Cloëon dipterum*). This nymph also absorbs oxygen through its body wall, but it flaps its gills in order to keep water moving past it. It creates its own little current, in fact, so as to be able to breathe. One Pale Watery—the Small Spurwing, or *Centroptilum luteolum* —has a remarkably adaptable swimming nymph. It can breathe

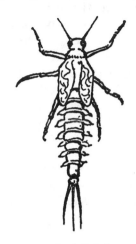

NYMPH
(of a typical
Ephemeropteran)

equally well in slow rivers, fast streams and lakes, so it is one of the commonest and most widespread flies in the country.

Other nymphs, which prefer other places, hardly swim at all but crawl slowly around the bottom of rivers and lakes. They usually have thicker bodies and stiff, strong legs to help them. Probably the best-known, at any rate to fishermen, is the Blue-winged Olive—*Ephemerella ignita*—which will make its home in almost any flowing water, acid or alkaline, and is the most likely fly to hatch in the evening on many rivers. Then there is the Claret Dun—*Leptophlebia vespertina*. This nymph can live in lakes, ponds or streams but it seems to prefer acid peaty water to alkaline water, which is a very rare liking for flies to have.

Another set of crawling nymphs is made up by the four species of *Caenis*, the Fisherman's Curse, the smallest of the Ephemeropterans and terribly difficult to imitate when it is on the water.

Other nymphs again cling tenaciously to rocks and stones and have developed flattened bodies so as to give themselves a firm grip. The March Brown—*Rhithrogena haarupi*—is a perfect example. It not only has a flat body, offering very little resistance to the current, but it also uses a suction arrangement, whereby it can make a vacuum between itself and a rock and so avoid being swept away even by the fastest streams. The March Brown is a river-dweller but the Yellow May Dun and August Dun—*Heptagenia sulphurea* and *Ecdyonurus dispar*—can both be found in rocky lakes as well. Both nymphs are flattened and can live in either fast or still water so long as it is not too acid and has the rocks and stones which they like.

The only nymphs that do not swim, crawl or cling are the Mayfly nymphs. They dig and burrow. Just as moles and badgers have developed strong forelegs for excavation purposes, so have Mayflies. They dig out little tunnels in the silt or mud of rivers and lakes and set up house in them. Like all flies which are capable of living in still water they can make their own current by using their gills.

So different waters contain different kinds of nymphs. They are usually vegetarians and feed mainly on the algae covering underwater plants or stones, and sometimes also on decaying plants at the bottom of the water. Their natural enemies are many and they have to beware of nearly any creature larger than themselves. Even tiny water mites eat the very young nymphs, while older nymphs make good meals for the larvae of dragonflies and stoneflies, as well as water spiders and—of course—fish.

Over a period the nymphs grow steadily. Every so often they moult and shed a complete outer case to make room for their increasing size. Inside each successive case the wings of the flies, non-existent when the nymphs first hatched from the egg, gradually take shape. Slowly the nymphs begin to look more and more like wingless versions of adult flies, until one day the time comes for them to hatch.

If fishermen could prophesy exactly when flies of a particular sort would choose to hatch, there would be a lot less time wasted by the riverbank. But nobody can. Water-temperature, air-temperature, atmospheric pressure and sunshine must all have something to do with it. Different flies seem to prefer different conditions. Iron Blues, for instance, nearly always hatch best in cold weather and Blue-winged Olives nearly always hatch best in the evening. But exceptions do occur and no-one, with all the thermometers and barometers in the world, has ever been able to guarantee that a hatch of so-and-so will take place between the hours of such-and-such.

When a quantity of flies of the same species decide to leave the water and take to the air, this is a fisherman's hatch. It should bring trout onto the feed. A few flies may hatch singly beforehand and afterwards but most of them are guided by some mass-instinct and choose roughly the same time. All over the river, or all over the lake, flies appear at the same moment as if summoned by a rallying-cry.

The nymphs hatch in different ways. Some species of fly climb out of their final nymphal cases below the surface, and then come up to the air surrounded by a film of gas to keep them dry. Others crawl out onto a stone or reed before they change from nymph to fly. But the majority of Ephemeropterans swim or float to the surface and hatch there. These mature nymphs usually have some air inside their skins to help them ascend and how it gets there is something of a mystery. Some swimming nymphs may pay a visit to the surface and swallow a gulp of air a little time before hatching, others may obtain it from dissolved gases in the water, and others by sucking it from the stems of reeds.

Once at the surface a nymph splits its case down the back and the adult fly struggles out. The crumpled wings, imprisoned for so long, soon expand in the warm air and after a flutter or two the insect is able to fly clumsily and laboriously towards the shore. The nymphal 'shuck' is left behind. Now the fly has entered the third stage of its life—that of a sub-imago, or dun. It no longer absorbs oxygen from the water through its body-walls, since the shedding of its case has revealed a series of very tiny air-holes underneath. Air filters in through these and oxygen is extracted from it.

A dun cannot eat or drink. Its mouth-parts are useless. This is one of the reasons why the lives of Ephemeropterans above the surface are so pathetically short. When they have hatched they take shelter in the neighbouring foliage, often on the undersides of leaves, and wait for their next and last transformation. If you search under the leaves by the side of a river you can nearly always find several sorts of duns sitting, resting and waiting. The time varies. Species of *Caenis* sometimes only spend a few minutes as duns before going into their fourth stage, Mayflies may take a few days, but most flies take about twenty-four hours or a little longer if the weather is cold.

Ephemeropterans are the only flies that change at all after becoming winged. The change consists of a further moult, when they shed one more complete skin, the whole outer covering of head, body, wings and tails. If you keep some duns in a jam-jar or butterfly cage you can watch them do it, and it is amazing to find that so delicate an insect can take off another entire coat. The fly that emerges is a 'perfect' fly—an imago—and is even more delicate than the dun. The colour of its body is sharper and brighter, its wings are more transparent and its tails and feelers are thinner and longer. It may have two tails or three tails. All Ephemeropteran nymphs possess three short tails, but when the fly eventually hatches it usually only has two longer ones. Some species, however, such as Mayflies and Blue-winged Olives, have three.

As soon as flies commence the last stage of their lives fishermen call them spinners. Again they wait under cover for a while, until the time comes for them to mate, and during this period their colours tend to alter slightly. The fly that finally mates may not look quite the same as a younger spinner and may bear practically no resemblance at all to the dun, except in size. A male Iron Blue Dun, for instance, is a dark steel-blue colour all over, while its spinner—the Jenny Spinner—is nearly all white except for a touch of dark-brown at the end of its body. All this is fascinating to watch but it makes the recognition of flies rather more difficult.

When the flies are ready to mate, and when weather conditions are right, they fly out from their shelter. Usually they choose fairly calm weather, or if the weather is windy they find protected places behind woods or bushes. The males and females have to meet each other. They do this by dancing. The males collect in swarms, sometimes of only a few flies and sometimes of thousands, and perform an aerial dance during which the swarm keeps roughly in the same spot unless it is swept away by a sudden breeze. The dance of most species consists of soaring up a few feet, then dipping down again, then soaring up again, and continuing like this for perhaps as long as several hours. Some species hover and do not really dance, but this is not so common and the very name spinner comes from the endless rising and falling of the dancing flies.

The females come upon these swarms and fly round the fringes of them until they can attract a male, or several males. The males then leave the swarm, pursue the female, and the successful suitor mates with her in mid-air. He has a tiny pair of forceps right at the end of his body with which he can hold her. Male spinners usually have a different colouring from female spinners of the same species, but often the presence of these forceps is the easiest way of telling a male dun from a female dun when they first hatch.

After mating the two flies sink down on to the ground, still joined firmly together. Soon they separate. They have not much longer left to live. The male may go back to join his swarm for a short time but he dies a little later. The female may take shelter again for several hours, or she may not. Then she flies off to lay her eggs.

Species of *Baëtis* crawl underneath the water, down a weed or rock or anything sticking up above the surface, in order to lay eggs. As they submerge a film of air sticks to their bodies to keep them dry. They normally lay their eggs on stones, where they are held by a gluey substance which covers them. Afterwards the spinners crawl or float to the surface, helped by their envelope of air. Some of the little creatures may then perish immediately and if not they are likely to die within a very few minutes.

Spinners of other species lay their eggs on the surface. Some of them sit on the water to do so, some release their eggs from

the air and some dip briefly down on to the surface to let
the water wash the eggs away from their bodies. The number
of eggs laid by these spinners may be anything from a few
hundred to several thousand according to the species. When
they have finished their job of egg-laying nearly all the female
spinners die exhausted on the surface of the water. They are
then described as 'spent' flies.

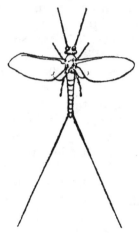

'SPENT' EPHEMEROPTERAN
(TRANSPARENT WINGS, LONG TAILS)

Trout have a chance to feed on Ephemeropterans at any
stage after they have hatched from the egg. They sometimes
hunt among the weed-beds for nymphs. Any nymph that
temporarily leaves its hiding place is in danger of being
snapped up. Perhaps the most dangerous time of all for nymphs
is when they make the ascent to the surface just before hatching,
because then they have no cover and are easy meat for fish
to catch. And even afterwards their troubles are hardly over.
Trout will usually be ready and waiting to rise and take
them while they hatch. Birds will swoop down to pluck them
neatly from the water. The same birds may take them in the
air before they can reach shelter, and again later on while
they are dancing as spinners. Finally the trout can feed on
the spent flies as they lie dead or dying on the surface.

Fishermen have almost as many chances to catch trout as trout have to catch flies. If the trout are feeding on nymphs below the surface, a fisherman can catch them on a sunken imitation of a nymph. If they are rising to a hatch of duns, he can catch them on an artificial dun, and when there is a fall of spinners he can use an artificial spinner. Occasionally trout feeding on a fly at one particular stage will refuse it at all other stages. So it is sometimes far more important to realize whether the fish are taking nymphs, duns or spinners than to recognize the exact species.

The Ephemeropterans are the mainstay of most dry-fly waters. Other types of fly, however, can be very useful too, and among them are the *Trichoptera*. The *Trichoptera*—usually called sedge-flies or caddis-flies—are quite easy to distinguish from *Ephemeroptera* because they never carry their wings upright but fold them back over their bodies like the roof of a house. The shape of a typical sedge-fly is shown in the picture below. There are nearly two hundred species of them in the British Isles, though only a few of these are of real interest to fishermen.

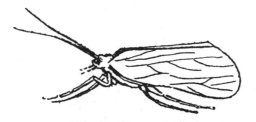

SEDGE FLY (HUMPED WINGS)

These sedge-flies also develop in four stages but unlike Ephemeropterans they go through three underwater stages and only one winged stage. The larvae, which correspond to the nymphs of up-winged flies, hatch from the eggs and live among the stones and plants of rivers and lakes. Many of them build themselves cases of sand, gravel, wood, leaves or whatever materials happen to be available. The cases give them some protection from attack and also provide excellent camouflage. Other species of sedge-fly, however, do not build

cases but live naked. While they grow the larvae feed not only
on vegetable matter but on small water animals and on the
eggs of other insects as well. They are voracious creatures
and so can cause a lot of harm amongst the eggs and young
nymphs of the up-winged flies.

After a little while the larvae go into a quiescent stage of
pupation. Each fly forms a pupa either inside its case or in a
silk cocoon which it spins for itself. Then it ceases eating and
hardly moves until it hatches. When that time comes, which

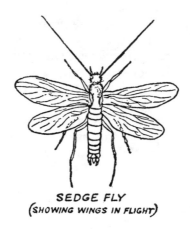

SEDGE FLY
(SHOWING WINGS IN FLIGHT)

may be after several weeks or several months, it tears open
its case or cocoon and swims up to the top of the water where
the adult fly climbs out of the pupa. Some species crawl ashore
to hatch and then of course the trout do not have such a good
opportunity to feed on them.

In the adult or winged stage sedge-flies will live rather
longer than up-winged flies because they are lucky in being
able to drink. This means they can obtain a little nourishment
and preserve their body-moisture. After perhaps a week or a
fortnight the males and the females will find each other.
The flies then mate at rest instead of in the air. Finally the
females fly off to lay their eggs either on the surface or by
crawling beneath it, and often float spent and dead on the
water after this is done.

Certain species of sedge-flies, such as Grannoms and Grey

Flags, only live in flowing water while others are equally comfortable in rivers or lakes. Their complete life-cycle may take one, two or three years. Trout feed on both the larvae and the pupae but these are rather difficult for a dry-fly fisherman to imitate. The hatching flies, the egg-laying flies and the spent flies all provide very good sport, however, and they have an extra advantage in that they sometimes stay on the water very late, long after other sorts of fly have vanished. On the chalk-streams, for instance, there is usually an evening hatch of Blue-winged Olives during the summer, and when this stops at dusk you can often catch trout for another twenty minutes or so on a sedge.

Stone-flies—the *Plecoptera*—look superficially not unlike sedge-flies, since they also fold their wings back. But they do

STONE FLY
(FLAT WINGS)

not hump their wings over themselves like a sloping roof, as the sedge-flies do. Most of them carry their wings quite flat, more like a level roof, while a few fold them closely round their bodies like a skin-tight garment. The wings of all stone-flies fit much more tightly than those of caddis-flies.

Nearly any type of water will support a number of stone-flies of various sorts but they are only really common in stony or gravelly river-courses or in lakes with stony edges. They vary in size considerably. The Large Stone-fly grows to well over an inch in length, while the Needle-fly, the smallest of the stone-flies, is only about a third as long.

Although the up-winged flies and sedge-flies have four stages of development, the stone-flies have just three—egg stage, nymph stage and eventually winged stage. The nymphs or larvae, when they come out of the eggs, crawl on the bottom among the stones and feed on the larger plants as well as on algae. The bigger species of stone-fly eat small animals. When the time comes all the nymphs crawl along the bottom, up the shore and onto dry land before hatching, a habit which means that trout can never take them on or near the surface as they can other nymphs.

The flies do not mate and lay their eggs until after two or three weeks. Like the sedge-flies they can drink and some species can even eat vegetation as well. Most stone-flies live for about a year in all. The very large ones are some of the longest-lived of water insects, because they take a full three years to develop. The females of all species lay their eggs on the surface and the times when stone-flies are most useful to fishermen are either while they are doing this or while they are dying on the water a little later. Then the trout may rise to them.

In many waters, among them the chalk-streams, stone-flies are of no real value because there are not enough of them. It is only where conditions are ideally suitable for them, as they are in rocky hill-streams, that the flies hatch abundantly and are worth imitating. But in strict contrast to this, the fourth and last major order of fisherman's fly—the *Diptera*— is the most wide-spread of all and large numbers of them are available to trout in any reservoir or stream. The most important members of *Diptera*, from the still-water fisherman's point of view, are the non-biting Midges or *Chironomidae*. They breed wherever there is water of any sort, even in the water of drinking-troughs, rain-butts and ditches.

There are usually plenty of Chironomids—or Midges—in

ponds, lakes and reservoirs everywhere. They are long-legged insects—the length of their legs is a helpful distinguishing feature—with pale wings a little shorter than their bodies. Many of them are a bit longer than the misleading name midge might lead you to suppose, and there are some species which reach a size of half an inch. They go through four stages—egg, larva, pupa, fly. The larvae are worm-like, without obvious limbs. Some of them are pale-olive in colour; others, frequently called blood-worms, are bright red in colour

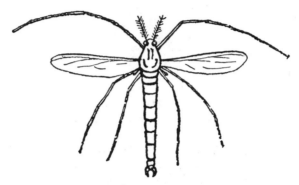

MIDGE (LONG LEGS, THIN BODY)

and can live on far less oxygen than any other water insect. In badly polluted water these blood-worms are often the only insects that flourish.

Whether the water is still or flowing, deep or shallow, acid or alkaline, midges of one species or another will be able to make it their home. A good many of the larvae like burying themselves in mud but others can be found almost anywhere. Some live only for weeks, others longer. The larvae pupate and the pupae swim up to the top of the water to hatch. The trout feed on the hatching pupae—which can be imitated—and sometimes rise also to the female flies when they lay their eggs on the surface.

The Chironomids are extremely useful on reservoirs and lakes where there are less flies of other sorts than in most rivers. In rivers, however, the *Simulium*—or Reed-Smut—group of *Diptera* is a more important part of a trout's food. Smuts, which breed in almost any flowing water, are very small, thick, stumpy flies with dark bodies and light wings which they carry in the same way as a housefly. Unlike the midges their legs are short. Fishermen call the slightly larger species Black Gnats and although the true Black Gnats—such as the species *Bibio johannis*—belong to a different group of *Diptera* and breed on land, they all look much alike and the same artificial fly serves to imitate them.

SMUT
(SQUAT BODY, STUBBY WINGS)

Smuts again pass from egg to larva to pupa to fly. They also live for varying periods. The larvae are little, pale, thin creatures, with one end of their bodies appearing to be slightly swollen, and they usually inhabit weed-beds in flowing water. There has to be a current, because the larvae get their food by straining it from the water through their mouths, where they have a tiny grid-like filter.

The pupae of smuts hatch out below the surface and the adults float up to the top completely enclosed in a bubble of gas so that they can fly away quite dry. They may be taken by trout at this stage, but the fish seem fonder of them when they are lying spent on the stream after laying their eggs.

That ends the list of the types of fly that are most interesting to a fisherman. The number of different species often sounds a little alarming at first. But the great thing is—as Part III tries to explain—that the variety of flies likely to hatch at any one time, on any one day, in any one place can be narrowed down to a very few, and it is usually possible to recognise these fairly quickly. There is luckily no need for a fisherman to carry a trunkful of flies—most of us clutter our flyboxes unnecessarily— nor need he keep a Latin dictionary.

PART THREE

CHALK STREAMS
AND OTHER WATERS

Chapter 8

Early Season

All through the winter, and even in early Spring, a river looks unfriendly—secretive—discouraging. You do not feel welcome there. Probably the colourful beauty of the valley around it has stayed in your memory long after your rod has been packed up at the end of September; but now, at the beginning of March, there is little promise of colour in the bleakness of the countryside. The bright, golden days of the previous summer seem a long way off, and you wonder if they will ever come again.

Even the chalk-streams, crystal-clear before, are sullen and swollen from the autumn and winter rainfall. They swirl along through drab meadows. If you peer into them you may not be able to see the river-bed except in the shallows. Even if you can, there are no trout to be seen and you begin to wonder whether there are any fish in the water at all. Perhaps it was over-fished last year? Perhaps some form of disease or pollution has killed the trout or sent them elsewhere?

The stream is depressingly bare of weed as well. There is not much left to remind you of those rich, food-producing beds of ranunculus and starwort that you cut with so much labour only a few months ago.

But even now, in rivers, streams and lakes all over the country, life is still carrying on below the surface. Tiny nymphs are growing steadily—not so fast as they will when the water temperature rises, but growing all the same—and getting closer to the time when they will hatch out. The trout have finished spawning and are waiting for food in their various hiding places. Heaven knows exactly where they hide themselves. When there is no food about, it is possible to walk along stretches of water that look as if they could not conceal a minnow, and never see a trout. Yet you know the fish are

79

somewhere there. Then, when the flies come onto the scene, you can look again and see four—five—six—seven trout all rising merrily.

At the moment, however, both trout and nymphs are waiting for more sun to bring out more water-food. Then the river will suddenly wake up. The sun will make the weed grow, the weed will collect algae, the algae will provide food for the nymphs, the nymphs will become strong and active, and as soon as they hatch the trout will feed on them greedily to make up the weight they have lost in spawning.

You may see a few Large Dark Olives hatching out on the chalk-streams in early March, with perhaps an odd trout splashing up to take them. They will not necessarily hatch best on the sunniest days. But only the sun can speed up the tempo of underwater life. In winter the tempo is rather slow and it must quicken before fishing can begin.

By mid-March, although there may be more insect-life about, the trout in the chalk-streams will still be recovering from spawning. They will be very thin. It is a shame to fish for skeletons when a few weeks will put flesh on them, so chalk-stream fishermen must wait till later on before starting the season.

Many other rivers and streams, however, open for trout-fishing on either March 1st or March 15th, and the trout in them are far plumper by that time. Some of them have wonderful hatches of March Brown, an early fly seldom found on any chalk-stream. Perhaps the Usk is the first really famous British river to come into condition, and here the March Brown will be in full swing during the last half of March and the beginning of April.

The March Brown can hardly be mistaken for anything else. It is a big, brownish up-winged fly. It has buff wings and a rather unpronounceable Latin name like a hiccup— *Rhithrogena haarupi*. If you forget the Mayfly, the March Brown is a very large fly for an Ephemeropteran, and it hatches incredibly suddenly. You may be staring at a blank stretch of water, where not a trout is rising. Then, a minute later, the air seems to be filled with clumsy dull-coloured insects, all fluttering on their way from the water to the shore.

The only trouble with the March Browns is that they often

stop hatching almost as suddenly as they start. Sometimes they only go on for about a quarter of an hour. So you have to make the most of them. This will hardly be the time for excessive caution. The trout, as early in the year as this, will be greedy and forgetful of the various dangers they learned about last summer. The best course is to tie on a March Brown quickly, cover as many fish as possible in the brief period of excitement and land as many as possible without delay.

When the fly stops hatching the river seems dead again. But there may be another hatch after a short time. In fact, there may be as many as three or four hatches of March Browns during the day, probably between eleven o'clock in the morning and three o'clock in the afternoon. If there are not, casting a dry fly into likely places may always bring up a fish or two. But a wet fly will probably be more successful. At the very beginning of the season, the trout are not really used to feeding on the surface, except on the March Brown. Some other flies may hatch but usually not very many. For most of the day, therefore, the trout are more likely to be looking for nymphs and grubs rather deeper in the water. So a wet fly reaches them better and can account for trout before, between and after hatches of March Brown.

When April comes, the chalk-stream season begins—though many chalk-stream fishermen wait till May—and it begins with the Large Dark Olive. This Olive is not quite so big as the March Brown, but it is another pretty sizable fly. It appears on a great many rivers, not only on chalk-streams, and has a dark olive-green body with dull bluey-grey wings. Among other names given to *Baëtis rhodani* in various parts of the country are Dark Olive, Large Spring Olive and Winter Olive. It is easily the most frequent fly on the chalk-streams at the beginning of April.

The most probable time of day for the Large Dark Olives to hatch is about one o'clock, but they may appear as early as eleven if the weather is warm and sunny, or as late as three if it is a cold day. Cold days never seem to discourage the Large Dark Olives hatching—I have seen these flies spreading their wings gaily in snow-showers—but cold often delays the process a little.

During an early Spring, you may well discover Medium Olives—either *Baëtis vernus* or *Baëtis tenax*—hatching out as well, as April wears on. If you see flies on the water with high dusky-coloured wings, those will be Large Dark Olives. The best artificial fly, then, will be a good Rough Olive, or a Blue Upright or perhaps a Dark Olive. If the natural flies are a fraction smaller, and rather lighter in colour, they are nearly bound to be Medium Olives. A good Medium Olive or an Olive Dun will do quite well, but over and over again a Gold-Ribbed Hare's Ear has proved itself an even more killing fly when Medium Olives are about. And then there is Greenwell's Glory—an extremely useful fly which serves for either a Dark or Medium Olive.

The nymphs of both the Large Dark and Medium Olives like living in very well-oxygenated water. Shallow, fastish water is better oxygenated than slow, deep, smooth water. This means that the shallows of a chalk-stream are better places to fish than the deeps during April. More fly will be hatching and wherever the fly hatches in strength trout will begin to feed.

One other possible fly in April is the Grannom. The Grannom, unlike the Olives, is a caddis-fly, or sedge-fly. All flies of this type, when they are not in the air, keep their wings folded back over their bodies. Grannoms also have a habit of struggling along over the top of the water, kicking up a bit of a commotion and leaving a wake behind them, instead of letting themselves be carried along smoothly by the current until they fly away.

The Grannom is one of the few sedge-flies which ever hatches *en masse*. It does not appear on all trout streams, but where it does the trout sometimes have a feast and fishing with an artificial Grannom can be very good.

Just occasionally there may be no hatch of fly at all. At these times your best hope lies in finding a trout feeding on nymphs. Even when they are not about to hatch, nymphs often seem to go through periods of activity which expose them to trout. These periods may occur when the nymphs themselves decide to feed or perhaps when they make mass migrations from one weed-bed to another.

If a trout is darting from side to side under the water, obviously feeding on something, he may take a sunk nymph. So it is well worth-while dropping one over him. Even when the trout is not in view you often see surface-signs of under-water disturbances—bow-waves, boils, humps or barely-distinguishable swirls—all made by nymphing trout.

Nymph-fishing, however, is an art in itself and there will be more to say about it later on. Early-season fishing on the chalk-streams has just one slight disadvantage. You cannot really have a day's fishing. All your sport will be crowded into a fairly brief period during the hatch. The Large Dark Olives may hatch for one or two hours and the Medium Olives for a little longer, so that if both these flies follow each other on the water you may have as much as three or four hours of good fishing. But you will seldom have more, because you will be unlikely to catch many trout before or after the fly is on the scene. The long-drawn-out hatches of mid-summer are still to come and there will be no evening rise till June. Another trouble is that even the trout you do catch may not yet be in perfect condition.

If I had my choice of rivers to visit in April, I should go to Scotland, or to the North Country, or the West Country, where the season starts earlier and the trout are fatter and keener. The March Brown will probably be over but the trout will have started to feed on the surface to other flies. They will be eager to take full advantage of floating food at almost any time of the day.

In the West Country, for instance, you can catch trout from after breakfast till sunset, and enjoy the open air and the country for as long as the sun is in the sky. The middle of the day will still provide the peak hours for the dry fly but there will be no time when you need consider yourself foolish to be fishing it. Besides, the wild daffodils and primroses and wood anemones during early spring in the West Country have to be seen to be believed. Not all your trout will be caught by chalk-stream methods. On the chalk-streams you usually wait till you see a rise and then you settle down to catch the trout that made it. On West Country streams such as the Tamar you can certainly do this with the trout you

spot rising but when there are no insects on the water you have
to go and search for the trout with your fly.

That is the main difference between the two sorts of fishing,
between the chalk-streams and other streams. On the Test
and Itchen and rivers like them food is so abundant that the
trout do not have to feed all day. When food is readily available,
during a hatch of fly for instance, the trout will feed well but
afterwards they will sink to the bottom of the river to rest and
digest, and nothing you can do will tempt them in the slightest.
But trout in streams like the Tamar are not nearly so lucky.
There is far less food.   They cannot afford to let any edible
morsel pass them by and so they are on the lookout practically
all day long.

Sometimes there are splendid rises on these streams. But
there is no cause for despair if not a single fish can be seen
breaking the surface. Even in those circumstances it is possible
to catch plenty of trout by 'fishing the water'—that is, by
casting a fly in promising places.

At the times when flies hatch, the trout will rise. You can
go from fish to fish, casting over each one with a good chance
of catching him. The trout rise a little faster than they do
on the chalk-streams, and you have to strike a little more
quickly. Among the likely flies to hatch will be Olives, sedges,
stone-flies and smuts.

The Olives are the same as the ones that hatch on the
chalk-streams. There may be a few sedges and stone-flies about
as well (though it is a little early in the year for many species
of sedge). If they hatch they can sometimes be seen not only
on the water but also in the air and crawling about on the
stones and bushes by the side of the river. They are easier
to identify when they are at rest. Both sorts of fly carry their
wings, not upright, but folded over their bodies. There is a
difference, however. A sedge's wings are humped over its
back like a little sloping roof while a stone-fly's are folded
much closer, usually flat and flush with the body or occasionally,
as with Willow-flies and Needle-flies, like a thin sheath.

Many sedges wait till the evening to hatch—but the Grannom is an exception, and so is the Grey Flag. Both hatch
during the daytime. There are three or four separate species

of sedge-fly commonly called Grey Flag or Grey Sedge. They vary in size but are all coloured grey, and the trout feed on them at several stages. They feed on the ascending pupae and hatching flies during the day and again on the spent flies in the evening, when they fall on the water after laying their eggs. The Grey Flag is a river-dweller rather than a lake-dweller and a Silver Sedge serves as a reasonable imitation of it.

Stone-flies offer fewer chances to the trout. They crawl onto land to hatch, which means that the only time when they are of any use to a dry-fly fisherman is after they have laid their eggs and died on the water. The trout, however, do feed on them while they are crawling along the bottom on their hatching journey, and many North Country fishermen enjoy great sport fishing with the live larvae or 'creepers'. These they collect from under the stones in the river.

It is worth-while keeping a watch for the odd stone-fly falling on the stream during April. The trout will take them. A Partridge and Orange or Grey Duster will catch trout when the Early Brown Stone-fly is about, and a good imitation of the Large Stone-fly may catch them when this unmistakeable, outsize, rather fearsome-looking insect is on the wing. Then there may perhaps be trout rising to Reed-Smut as well. On warm days, particularly in smooth water with a little shade, you may see four or five dimpling the water every other second, all within a few square feet.

These trout will be smutters. Each individual fly is so small that they have to work very hard to get a square meal out of them. A Black Gnat is probably the best fly here but often when the trout are fairly innocent they will treat an imitation of something larger as manna from Heaven and swallow it accordingly. I always try smutters with whatever fly I happen to have on my cast first, and then change to a Black Gnat if they will not take it. If you open the stomach of one of these trout you will find that it contains a huge black mass of partially-digested smut.

You can see that there is quite a variety of fly on a West Country stream in April, but they do not hatch so regularly as on the chalk-streams. Nor are the hatches so big. I have found on the Tamar, for instance, that I probably catch about half a daily bag of trout by casting to rising fish—perhaps more, perhaps less, according to the quantity of fly on the day—and the other half by casting a fly where trout may be lying, in fact by fishing the water.

Where *will* trout lie? To fish the river successfully a person has to be able to think like a trout. Where would you lie, if you were a hungry trout? Trout never like battling with the current if they can help it. They prefer to lie out of the direct force of the stream. But on the other hand it is the stream that brings them their food, so what are they to do? Like sensible creatures they compromise by finding some sheltered spot within reach and eyesight of a steady, not a raging current.

These sheltered spots can be provided by weeds, by rocks, by eddies and backwaters, and of course by dips in the riverbed. There is always shelter behind a rock. Also, perhaps less obviously, there is shelter in front of it. The current starts changing its course to by-pass or flow over a rock just before reaching it, leaving a cushioned space of water just upstream where trout often lie.

By watching the top of the water, you can learn how to 'read' the river like a book. Where two gentle currents converge, for instance, the food from both will be concentrated and a trout will probably be waiting. Where rough water changes to smooth, there will usually be a hollow in the riverbed. The stream will have dug out a lovely little resting-place for trout, from which they can dash to grab flies or anything else that comes down. If you put your fly over one of these hollows, however small it seems, you may well catch its tenant, or one of its tenants.

It is a sort of guessing-game, in fact, and you get better and better at it as time goes on. It is fun anyway. You work your way up the river, flicking your fly into all the places where you think a trout may be. Every now and then you will be right. A trout will nose up and your fly will go down and with luck the trout will soon be in the net. After a few days you make the pleasant discovery that you are getting far more rises and far more trout per hundred casts than you ever did when you started, because you are now beginning to think like the trout.

The trout will be less choosy and finicky than on the chalk-streams, and exact imitation of the fly on the water will not be so important. This is not to say that exact imitation can be completely discounted. A good imitation of the fly hatching will usually catch more trout than any other pattern. Some trout, however, will take an imitation of almost any fly. The local tackle-shop, wherever you are, will supply you with the most effective local tyings. Pheasant Tails and Ginger Quills are great stand-bys in many places. If you fish in fairly fast water they need to be tied rather larger than for chalk-stream fishing, because they can then be seen better on the ripples. Another good fly for rough water is the Grey Wulff, because it is tied with animal hair and floats excellently. Any of these flies is a good one to fish until a definite hatch takes place of some fly which you can imitate.

Rain-fed streams, subject to flooding, normally cut a pretty deep channel for themselves. When the winter floods are over, and the water-level goes down, the banks may be several feet high. This means wading. If you do not wade, you are so far above your fish that they can see you easily and will probably be frightened. So you get into the water in your thigh-waders and move cautiously upstream from fish to fish or from likely lie to likely lie, casting a short line. Once you are in the water you can get remarkably close to the trout.

These trout may seem small compared with chalk-stream or reservoir trout. There is a danger of chalk-stream fishermen and reservoir fishermen getting snobbish about the size of their fish. On the Tamar, for instance, the limit is eight inches and it takes three or four trout to make up the pound. On Dartmoor the limit is lower, only six inches. On several Irish streams that I have fished no trout are put back and they are all served up for breakfast next morning looking like a plateful of sardines. But even the smallest trout can be great sport. The answer is not to expect monsters. What you lose in weight, you make up in enjoyment and quality. And you never know whether your next cast may not produce a prodigious trout for the river, perhaps a trout of a pound or more, which would be nothing to be ashamed of even on the chalk-streams.

As a change from the dry fly there is always the wet fly.

When the water is clear the dry fly may account for more fish but when it is a little cloudy the wet fly may be as good or even better, The trout caught on the dry fly are usually larger. A wet fly sometimes seems irresistible to fingerlings and salmon-parr, some of which hook themselves quite badly so that you have to spend agonizing moments easing out the barb while the poor little fish wriggle about. Also, with the dry fly, you have the pleasure of actually seeing the trout take the fly.

Some experts in the West Country fish dry and wet at the same time and this can be a very successful method. They use two flies on their cast, a wet fly as a tail-fly and a dry fly half way up as a dropper. They cast upstream and the trout can take their choice. If they prefer the dry fly, the fisherman sees them rise. If they choose the wet fly, the dry fly acts as a sort of float which bobs visibly so that the fisherman knows when to strike. One of the great difficulties of fishing upstream with a wet fly is overcome—the fact that trout may take the fly without your knowing it.

Heavy rain is often the greatest enemy of the holidaying trout fisherman on a rain-fed stream. When the skies open and a downpour starts, salmon fishermen may be pleased because every spate brings up fresh, bright salmon from the sea. But all it means to the trout fisherman is coloured water in which even a wet fly fails to attract trout. That is when the locals go out and catch fine 'messes' of trout on the worm. The fly-enthusiast can do nothing except sit and twiddle his thumbs (unless he can fish a nearby lake) until the water clears. The higher up a river he is the sooner will fishing become possible again. The little tributaries clear first, within a few hours, then the upper stretches of the main stream and finally the lower reaches, which may take two or three days.

Once May starts, chalk-stream fishing really comes into its own. One great asset of the chalk-streams is that when you get up in the mornings you never have to scan the skies quite so anxiously. A strong downstream wind may make fishing tricky but rain will seldom make it impossible by clouding the water. This is because the chalk-streams are spring-fed. And by May the water-meadows are beginning to look really pleasant again. They will be greener and lusher than before, and there will be yellow king-cups and white ladies' smocks in them. Although the evening rise has not yet begun, Olives, Iron Blues and Black Gnats will be on the water for long hours during each and every day and spinners may fall in the late afternoon.

The Large Dark Olives will be over, but there will be plenty of Medium Olive hatches and there may be some Pale Wateries. The Greenwell's Glory and Gold-Ribbed Hare's Ear will again be good flies for the Medium Olive. It is not entirely clear why trout find the latter so attractive, though a possible theory is that the tying of the body may suggest a fly hatching out of its nymphal shuck.

Pale Wateries will hatch from the first warm days of late Spring till the end of the season. There are four flies commonly called Pale Wateries. They are: the Pale Watery itself (*Baëtis bioculatus*); the Small Dark Olive (*Baëtis scambus*); the Large Spurwing (*Centroptilum pennulatum*); and the Small Spurwing (*Centroptilum luteolum*). All, to a greater or lesser degree, look fairly 'pale' on the water—even the Small Dark Olive. The trout do not seem as fond of them as they are of the other Olives and the Iron Blues, but Pale Wateries will hatch on hot days when other flies will not. So they are a mainstay in warm weather. If the trout are taking small, light-coloured flies a Tups Indispensable or a Little Marryat should catch them.

There is also one important land-bred fly which falls on the water in May, though not in such numbers as in August, and that is the Black Gnat. May and late August are its favourite times, for it is never seen much in mid-summer. The Black Gnat—*Bibio johannis* and other species—is not an up-winged fly. When you notice tiny little dark bundles floating down the stream, with just a touch of white on their backs where they have folded their wings, these will be the Black Gnats that trout always seem to take so eagerly despite their small size. Usually, they take any good imitation of a Black Gnat just as eagerly.

But of all the flies that trout like perhaps the Iron Blue— *Baëtis pumilus*—is their favourite. The Iron Blue, again, is not a big fly. Its wings are blue-black, even darker than the wings of the Dark Olive, and its body is darker as well, so that from a distance it simply looks a small, jet-black, upwinged fly. When Iron Blues hatch out the trout usually decide to have a real feed and fishermen have a good day. Tackle-dealers sell both winged and hackled imitations of the Iron Blue. Tyings of the male fly often have a twist of red on the hook and I personally have a rather irrational feeling that this does attract more trout than the unrelieved darkness of the female fly.

Cold, windy, rainy May days lead to big hatches of Iron Blue, so that if the weather is hardly suitable for sunbathing the flies may provide plenty of compensation. Cold weather has another advantage, too. When nymphs hatch out into flies they stand on the water, supported by the surface-film, until their wings are firm and ready for flight. Then they take off. In warm weather this happens very quickly. But when there is no sun and the air has a bite to it, the flies stay on the water longer and the trout have a far greater chance to take them. More fish feed in consequence. All through the summer the fisherman has the best of both worlds. If the weather is fine he can enjoy it, but if it is not his fishing may be better.

Sedges are not very common on the chalk-streams in May, though the Welshman's Button—a smallish dark-brown sedge—sometimes appears on the water. Then an imitation of it may catch fish.

On lakes and reservoirs, the up-winged flies you see will not be the same as those on rivers. The most common ones to hatch in the first part of the season will probably be the Sepia Dun and Claret Dun (*Leptophlebia marginata* and *Leptophlibia vespertina*). They are large dark flies, about the same size as a Large Dark Olive—but they each have three tails, whereas the Large Dark Olive has only two. They can be imitated by a Sepia or Claret Dun—or by a Red Quill.

As late Spring approaches, Pond Olives (*Cloëon dipterum*) will begin to appear and will hatch throughout the summer. These are also darkish in colour, but a little smaller, and on close examination you will see that they have no rear wings. They have only two wings instead of four—a rare feature for any up-winged fly. Either a Rough Olive or a Grey Duster will imitate them.

Throughout the late mornings and early afternoons in May

fish should rise well. Warm, sunny days may bring out fly as early as half-past ten and a few fish may feed on nymphs preparing to hatch before the proper rise begins. On colder days neither fly nor trout may show themselves until one o'clock or two o'clock or even three o'clock. There is a record in my fishing diary of one day when I watched a lifeless river till five in the afternoon. Just as I was starting to go home in despair some Iron Blues began to hatch, then more and more. For two hours afterwards I had some of the best fishing of my life. I have never seen quite so late a hatch since that time but the memory of it has always helped me not to give up hope too early.

It is more common, however, to see falls of spinner than hatches of fresh fly in the late afternoon. Most spinners like dancing and laying their eggs best when there is not too much wind—but they do seem to prefer a slight, gentle breeze to a dead calm. In May, some spinners may lay their eggs and die in the morning and early afternoon but seldom in sufficient numbers to interest the trout. After tea there are usually more of them, often enough to make the trout take up their feeding-stations again. Spinners, unfortunately, are not at all obvious as they float down the stream on their last dying journey with their wings spread flat on the water. They are practically invisible except from directly above and the best sign of a trout taking spinner is his rise-form. When a trout takes an up-winged fly—a dun—he frequently sticks his nose up above the water. The rise is quite large. When he takes a spinner he does it far more gently, merely sipping it down from the top of the water. Occasionally he may skim it off the surface and show his back in a sort of roll but in neither case will a fisherman see very much of his nose.

So if trout seem to be rising quietly to invisible surface-food they are often taking spinner.

If you peer closely at the water beneath you, you can see the spinners floating down. They may be quite dead, in which case their wings will be outstretched, or they may have a little life left in them and still be holding their wings upright. Sometimes one wing becomes entangled in the surface-film, giving them a crumpled lop-sided appearance.

The different sorts of spinner can be told apart by their size and colour. This is not nearly so easy a business as recognizing duns because male and female spinners of the same species never look alike and both of them have changed considerably since the dun stage. However, the female spinners are really the only important ones. Most of the males die on land and do not fall on the water. Another lucky thing is that a comparatively small selection of artificial spinners seems to serve quite well for a large variety of natural insects.

The female spinner of the Large Dark Olive—sometimes called a Large Red Spinner—is pretty big and has a dark red body. The wings are colourless except for a few dark visible veins. An artificial Red Spinner imitates it very well.

It is more difficult to distinguish the spinners of other Olives, also those of Pale Wateries and some lake flies. Many of them have colourless wings and brown bodies ranging from dark brown to amber. Their exact colours vary a little from water to water and also according to climatic conditions. But if the spinners on the water—whether it be still water or running water—are fairly dark, a Lunn's Particular will imitate them well. And if they are light, a Little Amber Spinner or a Lunn's Yellow Boy will catch fish. A Pheasant Tail is another very good fly when Olive spinners are falling—and this includes the spinners of Pond Olives. (Many artificial spinners are tied with their wings stretched out so that they lie flat on the water and look like dead flies.) Fish often take artificial spinners more readily than they do the artificial duns, because a dead fly cannot flutter. A freshly hatched fly often does flutter, which is something that no artificial fly yet tied can imitate.

There is one spinner still left to describe, often the most successful of all. Trout love the spinners of the Iron Blue as much as the duns. The female Iron Blue spinner is a tiny fly with white colourless wings and a dark mahogany-red body. It looks just like an artificial fly called a Houghton Ruby and the Houghton Ruby is by far the best imitation of it. When these spinners are on the water you should catch plenty of fish.

You will find that early May is one of the best times on the chalk-streams. The trout rise freely. And the water-meadows become lovelier still as the month wears on. Now even the ashes

—those late-comers to the summer scene—will be busy covering themselves with leaves. Before long the hawthorn will begin to blossom and the ranunculus will push its white flowers up above the surface of the water.

But before then something else will appear on the surface, a large yellow insect, the lone vanguard of armies to follow. You will probably see a Mayfly.

Chapter 9
Mayfly Interlude

The Mayfly sometimes sends fish into frenzies of greed. But it can also send fishermen into frenzies of frustration. The only thing that can be predicted with any certainty at all about Mayflies is the approximate time of their arrival on the water. Whether Spring is late or early may make some difference. Even so, the Mayflies usually begin to appear on the water roughly when they are expected, within a few days.

However this time does vary from place to place. On the Lambourn in Berkshire, for instance, the Mayflies begin hatching well at the end of May. But on the Kennet—the river of which the Lambourn is actually a tributary—they seldom hatch until early June. The Mayfly season on the Test and Itchen starts between May 15th and May 20th. On some great Irish Mayfly loughs, where huge trout are caught by dapping with live Mayflies, the big hatches start in mid-May, but on others they start weeks later.

A fortnight or even more before the proper hatches begin, a few single insects will appear every day, and there will be little flurries of them in the second week of the fortnight. Fishermen will begin to roam optimistically up and down the river-bank, hoping for an early hatch. But if they try to fish with a Mayfly then, they seldom have much luck because the trout are not nearly so impatient. They will often feed on tiny Black Gnats in preference to the few succulent-looking Mayflies about. Even when the Mayflies do arrive in force the trout sometimes ignore them for a day or two. The first big hatches seem to frighten trout rather than attract them. They tend to treat the outsize insects rather warily, to leave them alone till they find out a bit more about them, and if possible to let the next-door fish do a little tasting before they feed themselves.

The small fish usually start rising to Mayflies first. Suddenly there will be an excited splash, and perhaps a second one, as an undersized trout comes half out of the water to grab a fluttering fly. Trout often rise to Mayflies with a splash, though the larger fish and the steadier feeders may take more quietly. These will be the trout worth catching.

And a truly thrilling sight it is when they come on the feed. Monsters, whose presence you may never even have suspected in the river, leave their hides and begin gulping down Mayfly after Mayfly. This is the real signal for a dry-fly fisherman. When big trout start feeding steadily, you know that it is time for a Mayfly to replace the Hare's Ear or Black Gnat on your cast. The Mayfly carnival is open at last.

Most fishermen find a sort of magic in Mayflies year after year. Here the life-history of many river-insects can be seen on a really grand scale. You can watch the stick-like nymphs come up to the surface and float there motionless for a few seconds until a split quickly appears down their backs. Through the split emerges a crumpled lump which then expands suddenly as if a mastless little boat had grown a sail in a few scant seconds. The whole insect struggles out of its prison, stands for a while on the water and then takes off clumsily, leaving the dead, useless, discarded nymphal shuck behind it. It flies badly at first. Perhaps it makes several landings on the water before it reaches the bank. Perhaps it never reaches the bank—since trout, swallows, swifts and so on take a heavy toll of hatching Mayflies. Watching these Mayflies hatch is rather like watching a fairy-tale unfold itself. It is a story of transformation and re-birth. The ugly, burrowing nymphs, who have spent at least two years embedded in silt and mud, suddenly gain the freedom of the air and are all changed into Prince Charmings and Beautiful Princesses. Every Beast becomes a Beauty. But they are only a short space away from the end of their lives. As nymphs they can feed but they cannot mate, and as flies they can mate but they have no mouths. They cannot feed. So your hatching Mayfly has made its choice between love and life.

These Mayflies provide many red-letter days. But a bad day is the most humiliating experience possible. This is what happens. You arrive at the water after breakfast to discover several trout lying near the surface apparently waiting for Mayflies. But no

Mayflies are hatching, so you decide to wait too. Nothing occurs till about three o'clock, when a few flies begin to hatch. The trout pay no attention to them at all. They do not seem interested. Apart from the fact that they have taken up feeding positions they might as well be asleep. You try casting over them but fail to bring them up. Then, about five o'clock, some more Mayflies float down the stream and all the trout immediately seem to go mad.

Before long there are fish splashing around on every side. The whole water is a scene of frantic activity with hundreds of Mayflies skimming over the surface and birds practically colliding with trout in their haste to pick them up. But somehow you cannot find a steadily feeding fish. As soon as you mark a trout he unaccountably stops rising. Nevertheless there are so many trout in evidence that you think you are bound to come across a regular feeder at some stage. And perhaps you do. You cast over him. He takes Mayflies to the right of you, Mayflies to the left of you, Mayflies all round you, but never your own fly.

Eventually you manage to deceive one innocent fish. He rises. You strike and miss him. The same thing happens again later, and yet again. Finally you begin to cast in a sort of panic, wondering why on this day of all days, when you should be reaping the Mayfly harvest, you cannot catch a single trout. Perhaps you never do, unless you foul-hook one who rolls playfully onto your fly in the course of his frolics.

There may be several reasons why a Mayfly day sometimes turns out badly. First of all a Mayfly is a very large mouthful for any trout. Many of them seem to like taking two or three May-flies one after the other, then waiting a little before coming back for a second helping. So the trout rise spasmodically. Then again a Mayfly, because of its size, is probably more difficult than other flies to imitate successfully. The shortcomings of the artificial may be very obvious. Often it is the struggling of the natural fly that fascinates trout. Occasionally they will let flies go by that make no movement, leaping to seize only those that flutter, and unfortunately nothing could look less like a lively Mayfly than the sodden bunch of feathers that you sometimes find on the end of your leader.

Again, trout frequently fail to get a Mayfly into their mouths, particularly when they rush at it excitedly. You often see them missing real Mayflies. At other times they seem to flop onto the natural flies without actually taking them, almost as if they were trying to drown them. So it is only to be expected that far fewer trout who rise to a Mayfly should be hooked than of those who rise to a smaller fly.

Of course none of these misfortunes occurs on a red-letter day. The trout rise consistently and steadily and it takes a great deal to frighten them. If you cast a Mayfly anywhere near them they grab it firmly. There is a great temptation to treat red-letter days as opportunities for slaughter. This is so wrong. They should really be days of big-game hunting, and the little fish who are so anxious to give themselves up can be left undisturbed to provide sport when the Mayfly season is over and done with.

The times of day at which Mayflies hatch are sometimes rather irregular. One day they may begin at ten o'clock in the morning but on the next the main hatch may not take place till six. There may be several hatches during the day or only one. Quite often the flies even hatch at different times on different stretches of the same river, so that while one fisherman is having good sport his next-door neighbour —a mere hundred yards or so away—may not be able to find a solitary rising fish. On a very, very good Mayfly day there may even be enough fly on the water from early morning till dusk to keep trout continually interested, with never a dull moment for any fisherman.

There are a bewildering number of Mayfly tyings in the tackle-shops. Some are hackled, others are winged and they range in colour from pale yellow to the darkness of the Black Admiral. It seems amazing that so many different patterns should be supposed to imitate only two natural flies—for there are two normal species of Mayfly, very similar to each other indeed— but nevertheless they all seem to catch fish on good days. On bad days perhaps none of them will. Local advice is usually the best to take on which pattern to use. It is probably worth buying several different sizes as well, because if one size is consistently refused a smaller or larger one may easily work better.

Mayfly nymphs live in silt or gravel and they will thrive equally well in still or running water. This is because they create their own oxygen-flow. They burrow into the silt at the bottom of lakes and rivers and keep water flowing through their little tunnels by fanning their bodies with their gills. In fact, on many slow, deep pieces of water, where silt has been deposited, the Mayfly season is the only time of the year when dry-fly fishing is any good at all. Conditions there are probably not suitable for smaller flies, except for midges and some sedges, but when the Mayflies hatch the big trout do come up to the surface.

Some lakes, particularly in Ireland, have tremendous hatches of Mayfly. You can fish these lakes—usually from a boat—in the normal dry-fly way by casting your fly in the path of one of the huge trout you see cruising around. Or you can fish by dapping. In order to dap, you need a long rod of twelve or fourteen feet, a light blow-line, a hook, a live Mayfly and a breeze. The live Mayfly is impaled on the hook. You then let the breeze blow it out on the blow-line until you can touch it down on the surface of the lake. No part of the line or leader should lie on the water. You watch your Mayfly dancing on the wave. Then a seven-pound trout takes it under. You curb yourself, for when you dap you must not strike quickly. So you close your eyes, recite a long prayer in Gaelic, and tighten. Afterwards, if you are lucky, you may find yourself with what appears to be a bucking horse at the end of your line.

After the Mayflies have been hatching on the river for about a week the great evening dances of Mayfly spinners begin. The flies, having shed a coat, come out from the trees and bushes to dance and mate. A big Mayfly dance is an awe-inspiring sight. The spectacle may start at any time from four o'clock onwards. A little cloud of male spinners comes onto the stage, looking now like graceful aerial acrobats, instead of the clumsy fliers they were when they first hatched. They dance over the water, or over the meadows by the side of the stream, soaring up and down in their thousands.

Round the males the females dance singly. Every now and then a male will leave the corps-de-ballet, fly towards the female he has chosen and attach himself to her. For a while they fly locked together in the air and then they sink down into the grass. Very shortly afterwards the female takes wing again to lay her eggs on the water, where she eventually falls exhausted. She becomes a spent fly. In the meantime the male flies off as

well and may even rejoin the dancers but only for the few
moments left to him before he also dies.

Most of the males die on land but nearly all the females die on
the water. They fly close to the surface, dipping down now and
again so that they just brush the stream and a cluster of eggs is
washed off their bodies, a few at a time. The eggs sink slowly to
the bottom where they will hatch into nymphs in future days.
As the afternoon wears into evening, more and more Mayflies
come to join the dance. Soon the air is full of them. I have known
evenings when you could not see more than a few yards for
Mayflies, when they alighted in hundreds on your coat, on your
trousers, all over your body, and when all you could hear was
the thin, brittle clatter of thousands of small wings. The sheer
quantity of them can be stupefying.

Nature appears to be in a wasteful mood. Here are countless
millions of female Mayflies all in the process of egg-laying. They
will lay wherever they can find room or wherever there is water.
They will lay in ditches and puddles, and if it has been raining
they will lay on the wet, gleaming surfaces of roads. All these
eggs will die quickly since they need oxygen even before they
hatch into nymphs.

Female Mayflies lay about six thousand eggs apiece. Even if
these are laid where they have some small chance of living, as
they normally are, very few ever reach maturity. Some become
covered with mud and literally choke. Most of them are eaten
by insects or small animals before they hatch out into flies.

It is a somewhat sad sight to see all the dead, spent Mayflies
floating downstream after egg-laying. Expressions like 'You
could walk across the river on them' seem very nearly credible
when you look at these Mayflies drifting down in dense masses,
wing-tip to wing-tip, with scarcely a glimmer of water between
them. Fishing is useless, since what hope has your fly among so
many? At the end of the evening the dancing flies have disappeared but the banks of the river are littered and piled high
with corpses. Weed-beds are covered with them, weed-racks are
blocked by them, until by dusk the whole stream is one vast
open graveyard for Mayflies.

Luckily, these tremendous Mayfly dances do not happen
every evening nor does every river support such large quantities

of fly. If they did, fishing with the spent Mayfly would not provide such good sport as it nearly always does. Usually when the Mayfly season is a week or so old, and the Mayfly spinners begin to dance, your chances of catching trout are practically doubled. You can catch them every day while the fresh flies hatch and again while the spent flies fall. A perfect evening should bring out enough spinners to keep the fish feeding on them well but not so many that you have to stand with a useless rod in your hand and watch the trout taking one fly in every hundred.

For some reason the imitation of the Mayfly spinner is called a Spent Gnat. It is certainly spent, but it is certainly not a Gnat. Often you find fresh Mayflies and spent Mayflies coming down the river at the same time, and then the trout may be feeding on both—or on only one of them. In the latter case it pays to watch carefully and find out which.

Mayfly spinners are easy to distinguish from fresh flies when they are finally dead and floating with their wings flat. But sometimes when they are still dying and have their wings upright, they look rather like the fresh flies. That is, in shape. Their colours are quite different. In the air, with the light shining through it, a Mayfly spinner looks beautiful, but on the water it looks almost dirty. The wings have dark veins in them and the body is grey, becoming brown near the tail. Even from a distance it can be told by the fact that it appears much darker in colour than a freshly-hatched dun.

Not nearly so many fish are pricked or missed during a fall of spent Mayflies as they are during a hatch of fresh duns. The flies are not fluttering at this stage, so a trout tends to take each fly more deliberately and steadily. You seldom see trout missing the natural spinners, while they often miss the fresh flies. If too many spinners fall on the main stream for good fishing, the side-streams and carriers may be better. There are usually less Mayflies in these little streams so that the trout in them are more ready to take every single fly that comes down.

Mayflies hatch properly for a fortnight or a little longer. When are they at their best? Major Waller Hills, in his book 'Summer on the Test', put forward the theory that the fourth and twelfth days were the most likely for a big basket. So far as any theory in fishing can prove itself correct, this theory does. He explained that on the fourth day the trout had become accustomed to the Mayflies and were no longer wary of them, but on the other hand they were not yet gorged. And by the twelfth day they began to sense that the hatches were falling off and were determined to make the most of them while they lasted.

Even in the middle of the Mayfly season it is a great mistake to ignore the smaller flies. They can be very useful on many days. Before the Mayflies start hatching in the morning, the trout often rise to a small fly far better than to a Mayfly. And I can remember one evening when Mayfly spinners were falling and the trout were rising furiously and I could catch none of them on a Spent Gnat. I eventually discovered they were not feeding on Mayflies at all, and when I changed rather belatedly to a Lunn's Particular I immediately began catching fish.

The Mayfly is not an unmixed blessing to fishermen. Wherever Mayflies hatch, and wherever the trout feed well on them, there is always an aftermath in summer when the Mayflies have gone and the gorged trout seem contemptuous of smaller flies. They often sink down to the bottom of the river, pay no attention to the hatches of Olives and Iron Blues, and only come up again much later in the season. That is always the trouble with Mayflies and many fishermen prefer a stretch of water where there are no Mayflies at all, because sport throughout the summer is less of a boom-and-slump affair. But nevertheless, who would be so foolish as to refuse an invitation to fish the Mayfly in its season?

Chapter 10
Nymph-Fishing and the Evening Rise

Nymph-fishing consists of catching a trout on an imitation of a fly before it has hatched. The imitation has to sink below the surface of the water, since that is where the natural nymphs will be. So nymph-fishing is perhaps not dry-fly fishing in the truest and strictest sense of the term. In a way it is more akin to wet-fly fishing, because whenever a trout takes a sunken wet fly (as opposed to a large and brightly-coloured 'lure') he usually does so under the impression that it is some underwater creature, probably a nymph. In fact, dry-fly purists used to denounce nymph-fishing roundly, as being an unfair way of catching well-bred chalk-stream trout. Some of them also carried on a long argument with the man who first recognised and wrote about all the enjoyment and success to be had out of this form of fishing—Mr. G. E. M. Skues. But Skues stuck firmly to his viewpoint. He said that an artificial nymph was a fair imitation of a natural insect, exactly as a dry fly was.

And of course he was right. By now the nymph is established as a skilful and perfectly legitimate way of catching trout on most stretches of the chalk-streams, and nearly everywhere else besides. But since nymph-fishing is still frowned upon on a few dry-fly-only waters, it is always wise to find out the local rules about it before fishing anywhere.

A nymph will certainly not catch trout at all times. It is a specific medicine, on the chalk-streams anyway, for those trout who are actually taking natural nymphs. It does give a fisherman a chance to fish with some hope of success for these trout, when they refuse duns. Before a rise starts trout may spend a little time feeding on nymphs. And if the hatch is very sparse they may find better feeding below the surface than on the surface. And some trout seem to prefer nymphs to duns even when there is a good hatch. When you examine the stomach-contents of trout it is amazing how many nymphs you nearly always discover in them, which shows that trout may often treat nymphs as their bread-and-butter and duns merely as jam.

This is not really surprising, because although trout have no control over hatches of fly at all, they can always go and hunt for nymphs in the weed beds when they feel hungry. In waters where plenty of duns hatch, and at the times of the year when they hatch frequently, trout will usually come to the surface to feed. But in waters of a different sort, or during weather when duns will not hatch, nymphs may become their staple diet. Many of these nymphs will be eaten by trout who are grubbing around deep in the weed-beds, or among the stones at the bottom of the stream, and are therefore seldom visible, even less get-at-able. Many other nymphs, however, will be swallowed more or less in the open by trout waiting for them to be brought down by the current.

When the nymphs are just about to hatch, or actually in the process of doing so, trout can often make a good meal of them. Then the nymphs come up to the surface of the water, break their way through the surface-film and float there for a short time while they hatch. Just a word here about surface-film. Water in contact with air always tends to cling together on its outer surface. It forms a film, which is why needles can be floated on water. There is always a surface-film on the top of a lake or river. In a way this is a help to insects, because they can stand on it, walk on it and generally treat it as humans might treat ice-covered water. It will support any small water-resistant object, such as a dry fly. But nymphs sometimes have difficulty in breaking through it and duns may become entangled in it, so that they cannot fly away. Scum on the surface often traps flies before they succeed in taking off.

While nymphs are on or near the surface-film and in the process of hatching, trout find them easy to catch. The nymphs are without cover and in full view of the fish and, although they may struggle a little, they do not flutter like a dun nor dart sharply through the water as swimming nymphs do at other times. So the trout take them quietly, without fuss or excitement.

If the nymphs are floating on top of the surface-film, a trout's rise may be rather like a rise to a spinner. But often the trout takes the nymphs before they get to the surface, and then his rise may not be visible at all. Occasionally you may see a small hump or boil—but frequently not even that.

Trout also feed on nymphs which are not necessarily going to hatch straight away, but which have temporarily left cover. The nymphs may be making a migration from one weed-bed to another. Or, if weeds have been cut, they may be escaping from drifting strands of it to a safer home. Or again, when they themselves are feeding, they may become rash and get swept away from their own weed-beds by the current. The trout are never slow to seize their opportunity to intercept the nymphs. These nymphs, however, are not all immobile. Some species make quick, spasmodic dashes through the water, so that the trout have to chase around and pursue them.

So trout, here, are frequently very active. They may move quite a long way from their original place to snap up the swimming nymphs. In shallow water they may give away their presence by plunging and flouncing about, leaving boils and bow-waves behind them. In deeper water, where they make no disturbance on the surface, they are usually more difficult to detect. The best hope, then, is to catch sight of the nymphing trout himself, which can often be done in clear, or fairly clear, water. The trout will probably be moving quickly and purposefully from side to side, opening and shutting his mouth from time to time as he takes a nymph.

Any of these nymphing trout may conceivably take a dun. But again they may not. If they are concentrating solely on the nymphs, it may be a waste of time to throw floating flies over them. Many a nymphing trout has been bombarded for hours with dry flies, to the complete disappointment of the fisherman concerned, who usually says afterwards: 'He *seemed* to be feeding well, but I just couldn't interest him'. That is why it is so helpful to be able to tell when a trout is taking nymphs, not duns. Even if you are fishing on water where the nymph is not allowed, you will at least know that here is a fish over whom you should not break your heart, and upon whom you should not spend all day, since he is unlikely to pay any attention to you.

Where the nymph is allowed, you have a fair chance of catching the trout. The selection of an artificial nymph should by rights pose a problem—since you will have no idea which species of nymph he appears to be so keen on—but in practice you will find that good all-round patterns usually work well. The Pheasant Tail and Grey Goose nymphs devised by Frank Sawyer are highly successful on most streams.

A nymph has to sink, and this can be greatly helped by the way in which it is tied. A nymph should be dressed very lightly, for otherwise it will offer too much resistance to the surface-film and will never slip through easily. Many artificial nymphs are now 'weighted'—usually by winding fine wire round the body— to make them sink more quickly.

If your nymph is not 'weighted' it sometimes sits stubbornly on the surface-film without sinking. Then a little fish-slime (or saliva) will help it to go under. By the time it reaches the trout it should be down to the level at which he is feeding—this needs nice judgement. The farther upstream you cast, the deeper it will sink before it reaches the trout. In a fast current, too, you must cast farther up than in a slow current. To stop the nymph sinking too deep, it is a good idea to grease the whole of your leader except for the last few inches.

A dragging nymph frightens trout far less frequently than a dragging fly on the surface, partly because it makes no wake— and partly because many natural nymphs make little darts and dashes through the water. In fact, if you cast your nymph within the range of a feeding trout and he refuses it, try jerking it deliberately next time. He will often have it. This technique has come to be called the 'induced take' and it accounts for many trout.

When a trout accepts an artificial nymph, the fisherman has to strike as he would with an ordinary dry fly. This is perhaps the most skilful and fascinating part of nymph-fishing. The skill lies in knowing exactly when to strike, and the fascination in finding an extremely firmly-hooked trout on the end of the line afterwards. Of course there is no difficulty about it, or very little, when the trout makes a well-defined hump or boil on the surface, but sometimes he takes the nymph very quietly beneath the surface, giving no clear indication of a rise. You have to watch the water like a hawk for the various signs which may mean the trout has the nymph in his mouth.

The most useful—and most reliable—of these signs is the

motion of the nylon where it goes into the water a few inches from the nymph. If you watch it carefully, you can see it travelling downstream at the pace of the current, until a trout takes the nymph, when it stops dead and then twitches or draws through the water as the trout moves down or away. The best time to strike is when the leader first stops, rather than when it draws, because in the first case the trout has seized the nymph in his mouth, while in the second case he is making off with it and may open his mouth at any time to get rid of it. For a fisherman with reasonably good eyesight, the checking of the leader is an invaluable message to say that a trout has found the nymph acceptable. Sometimes, admittedly, the nymph turns out to be caught up in some weed, but a few false alarms are far better than failing to strike when a trout does take the nymph.

Another message is the flash of a trout's flank or belly as he turns. Occasionally, as you gaze at the water where you think your nymph may be, you spy just the faintest glimmer of yellow and raise your hand to discover that you have hooked a trout. Skues called this the 'wink under water'.

If the trout is in full view, the fisherman may see him swim towards the nymph—or towards the place where the fisherman thinks the nymph is—open and shut his jaws and then turn to go back to his original position. Sometimes you cannot see the movement of his jaws, but the time to strike is at the precise moment of the trout's turning, not before. Then he is most likely to have his mouth shut, with the nymph inside it. The temptation to strike too early is very great. Whenever a trout can be seen coming towards a fly, an anxious person is only too liable to jerk up the rod-tip while the fish is still several feet away. A trout often follows a nymph for some way before seizing it, and it is all too easy to strike while the nymph is still only being inspected. As soon as he has taken it, he usually turns. So a wave coming along the surface of the water in the general direction of a fisherman's nymph is never a good signal to raise the rod. The trout is probably still approaching the nymph. When the wave starts to swirl and change direction, then is the time to strike.

Nymph-fishing is a very satisfying affair—when you see the sudden stopping of the leader, tighten at this slenderest of hints and then feel the rod bend in response. The sequence requires even more vigilance, if perhaps a little less delicacy, than to hook a fish taking duns. An advantage of nymph-fishing is that it gives you a second string to your bow. A fisherman with a nymph in his fly-box need never sit around in despair when there are no flies hatching. Even though no trout are rising at the surface, one or two may always be feeding on nymphs, and can sometimes be caught.

The nymph can be deadly on reservoirs as well as rivers. Patterns here tend to be a little more varied, and so are the different ways of fishing them. For instance, there are some patterns imitating small midge-pupae and these should be fished in or only just below the surface-film, which means greasing the leader right up to the end. Other patterns can be fished deeper. When you fish a nymph in still water you cast it out and then 'retrieve' it by drawing in line with your left hand. On occasions a fairly fast retrieve will catch trout. But often the best retrieve is a very slow and patient one—a little twitch every ten seconds or so. Brightly-coloured lures which imitate small fish are on the whole most attractive when they move quickly. But natural insects do not break speed records and artificial nymphs should seldom be hurried through the water.

Now for the evening rise. Once summer has started, this is another saver of many blank days. In flaming hot weather, when not a fly has appeared on the water all morning and all afternoon, fishermen usually look forward eagerly to the evening, because the evening rise may be especially good. The hotter the day, the better the evening rise. Your sport may be fast and furious. You may catch several fish in a remarkably short time. You may land one of the huge fish who never condescend to rise during the daytime. You may do wonders. Or—you may find yourself getting more and more frustrated as the light fades and your time runs out. You can easily cast over dozens of rising trout for a frantic and quite fruitless half-hour, and go home disappointed at the end of it.

Trout sometimes seem to behave very illogically during the evening rise, as they may do during a hatch of Mayfly. But the evening rise seldom lacks for excitement, and whether you catch trout or not, it is always cheering to see them show themselves just before dusk. The evening rise is probably the most regular meal-time that the trout have. Even on apparently perfect fishing days, flies may not hatch in the morning and afternoon, but there will usually be a rise of some sort in the evening, from mid-June onwards.

On reservoirs the dry fly often comes into its own in the evening. During the day you may see few rises, and the few that you do see may be out of reach, but in the evening the trout often cruise close to the shore, showing themselves as they take surface-food. Even though lures, wet flies and nymphs may have been all that would catch them previously, a dry imitation of a midge or a sedge—or perhaps of a tiny *Caenis*—can do much damage at dusk.

On a river the overture to the evening rise normally starts about an hour before the sun dips below the horizon. Very few up-winged duns will be on the water then, but a good number of spinners should fall as long as the wind is not too strong. Some of the spinners may belong to the ordinary daytime species of fly. The most frequent spinner to visit the water on a summer evening, however, is the spinner of the Blue-winged Olive— *Ephemerella ignita*.

This fly—a highly important evening fly—is common in rivers and streams all over the country. It occasionally breeds in big lakes too. The female spinner is a palish brown and this has led to its rather apt name of Sherry Spinner. On the right sort of evening you can see thousands of these Sherry Spinners winging their way upstream in long columns to lay their eggs.

They make a very pretty sight against the light, and a very reassuring one, because they will soon fall spent on the water and the trout will rise to them. The artificial Sherry Spinner is an extremely effective fly when trout are feeding on the naturals, so much so that a fisherman often catches more during this time than during the evening rise proper. Sometimes the trout ignore the duns when they do eventually hatch, and go on taking spinners for as long as they fall. The Sherry Spinners seem to prefer calm evenings for their egg-laying, or evenings with a very slight breeze.

Just as the sun begins to vanish, or perhaps just after its upper rim has disappeared, duns often start hatching. On the chalk-streams, they will probably be Blue-winged Olives, flies with three tails, olive-coloured bodies and distinctively high, blue-grey wings. Less frequently they may be Yellow Evening Duns (*Ephemerella notata*), or Pale Evening Duns (*Procoleon pseudo-rufulum*)—the former of which is a yellow three-tailed fly, while the latter is a medium-sized fly with two tails and no hind-wings. Unless, and this is unlikely, the river is slow-flowing enough to harbour Pond Olives, the Pale Evening Dun is the only fly you are likely to find with only two wings.

Imitation can be tricky. There is no sure fly for the evening. When the Blue-winged Olive is hatching, most fishermen use an Orange Quill—largely because that grand old man Skues advised it. Although it may be heresy to say so, I have seldom found it very much use. Yes, it will occasionally catch a trout or two but for my money I believe a Kite's Imperial is rather better. There are artificial Yellow Duns and Pale Evening Duns to match Yellow Evening Duns and Pale Evening Duns. You can also use a Little Marryat to imitate the latter.

If there is a good hatch, many more trout usually feed than are ever seen during the day. But this is where the silly cussedness of the evening rise comes in. Often the river seethes with trout. In every square yard, you see a fish rising well. It seems impossible that they should not take an artificial fly and come to the net, one after another. Yet you cast to fish after fish, fighting a hurried and losing battle against the fast-approaching darkness, without being able to make one of them so much as notice your fly, let alone take it. Since a trout has better eyesight in dim light than human beings have, it may be that against certain sorts of sky he can perceive the artificiality of an artificial fly even more clearly than by day.

But this does not always happen. Trout may give themselves up readily while the flies hatch. A hatch of Blue-winged Olives seldom lasts longer than half-an-hour, and it may only last ten minutes. Then there will be no Ephemeropterans left on the water. But the fisherman need not go home yet, because there may well be more excitement to come. After a short lull, or even without any lull at all, he is very likely to hear a heavy-sounding splashy rise somewhere in the stream—which will mean that there are some sedge-flies about. It is usually worth waiting ten minutes or so to see if the trout begin to feed on sedges. One chalk-stream keeper I know always used to complain to me that whenever a sedge-rise started none of his fishermen could be found and all he could hear was 'the slamming of car-doors all around'.

Sedge-flies stay on the water later than Ephemeropterans. When the bats begin to appear, that is the time when trout, including big trout, may come up for sedges. Some of these large old trout may hide themselves for most of the day, only leaving their holts under the cover of darkness. The greater part of their food will probably be made up of young trout, minnows, crayfish and other fair-sized items, but they are often prepared to take a sedge. Very large trout are often caught at sedge-time.

So it is a good idea to tie a sedge onto the cast, holding the eye of the fly up to the light, before it gets too dark to do it at all. Most ordinary sedge-patterns are quite effective, a Cinnamon Sedge being one of the most popular. When trout take spent sedges, they do so very quietly. But when the sedges are hatching or laying their eggs, the trout splash and slash at them, because they scutter across the top of the water. At these times it often pays to drag the imitation deliberately. Trout who ignore the fly when it floats normally sometimes wallop up to it viciously when they see its wake.

There is one other rule which the sedge-fly allows you to break. On the chalk-streams people usually fish for rising trout, and seldom cast a random fly, but a sedge at dusk is a permissible exception. It is often worth searching the river, or parts of the river, with a sedge when trout are not rising. But you have to know where the good trout are. Once you know the right spots, where the fish feed at dusk, you can frequently bring up some unexpectedly large fish. There is one particular stretch of the Itchen, just below a mill in the town of Winchester itself, which has very few Ephemeropterans in it. You seldom see a trout rising there. However, if you fish a sedge on this water in the late evening, you may well catch a trout of over two pounds.

While I am on the subject of large fish, I really cannot resist telling the tale of the largest wild trout I ever met. He lived in a culvert, through which flowed a tiny stream, the merest ditch, only three yards wide and a couple of feet deep. It formed one of the headwaters of the Itchen. Up above the culvert were some watercress beds and a good many shrimps from them were washed downstream to provide rich feeding for trout where the flow concentrated in the culvert itself. I came upon this place when it was almost dark, and immediately below the culvert I could just make out a long dark shape lying on the pale gravel.

As I watched, the shape tilted up to take something by the side of the brick wall. My first cast was not a brilliant one, but luckily my sedge chanced to touch the brickwork and dropped off right onto the trout's head. The shape tilted again. I struck, and the next moment my reel was giving out line as the trout ran up the culvert. There he stayed doggedly. He wouldn't budge an inch, and there was little enough I could do to bring him back. Only an occasional throb on the line reassured me that I was not snagged. After about three minutes of this, he came back towards me. Then he swam round for some time in stately circles—and I saw him once or twice. I thought he was a very good fish—at least three pounds. My main worry was that a large tuft of floating weed had somehow become attached to the 3X leader.

After about ten minutes in all, the fish was ready for the net, and I realized for the first time just how big he was. The only way I could possibly accommodate him was to draw the net over his tail, and on up his body, till only his nose was outside. The frame of the net broke as I lifted him up the bank, but the mesh held and soon I had carried him safely at least twenty yards into the field. I killed him quickly but then had to wait another five minutes before my hands stopped shaking enough to remove the hook. The fish weighed seven pounds and one ounce, and I do not suppose I shall catch so large a wild trout again. One advantage of catching a large trout like this is that it satisfies the more ambitious side of your nature. You are happier with small fish ever after. You no longer have to hope desperately, every time you go out fishing, that the trout of a lifetime will be around the next corner. You have already caught him. Whether you fish for six-inch trout in Scotland, or eight-inch trout in Devon, or two-pound rainbows in a reservoir, it makes no difference at all so long as the fishing in interesting. It is a great thing to catch one large trout.

Chapter 11

A Summer's Day

People who want to fish while they are on holiday seldom go in
the middle of the summer except for family reasons. The early
season is a better time for a fishing holiday. So is September—
but you often hear July and August referred to as the 'dead
months'. How true is this?

Where the Mayfly has come and gone again, fishing does
tend to deteriorate immediately afterwards. But where there
has been no Mayfly, good fishing may go on as long as the big,
concentrated hatches of small fly last, probably until the end of
June. For instance the first weeks in June are the best weeks of
the whole year on the Upper Itchen, with magnificent hatches
of Olives and Iron Blues. June is also very good on many rocky
streams where the water is cold and the river-bed is unsuitable
for Mayflies.

As the month draws to its close, however, the daytime hatches
of fly begin to fall off. The flies will go on hatching throughout
the summer, but with nothing like the same regularity, and
seldom in the same numbers. The water-temperature rises.
Streams, lakes and reservoirs are lower in depth, lower in
oxygen. You will not often see a mass display of trout till the
evening.

But daytime fishing in high summer is far from hopeless and
it can be very enjoyable. There is scarcely ever a time when it is
quite impossible to catch a good trout. The countryside looks
lovely during July and August and the banks of well-fished
rivers are less crowded. The gentlemen from the cities who came
down for easy Mayfly fishing have climbed into their large cars
and driven away. The river valleys have an air of luxurious
peace and all through the long warm days, however bad the
fishing may be, every fisherman can be buoyed up by the

thought that the breathless excitement of the evening rise is still ahead.

Trying to catch trout under difficult summer conditions is something of a challenge. And success is all the more rewarding. At this time a dry fly may succeed in streams where wet flies usually reign supreme. Anyone fishing a downstream wet fly in low, clear water is likely to scare most of the trout long before they see his fly. But if he keeps low and casts a delicate dry fly to his trout from behind, he may get some well-deserved results.

Except on the chalk-streams you will probably not see a great many trout rising in the heat of the day, but there are usually one or two. A few Pale Wateries should hatch even in the warmest weather, while cold rainy days may induce some Olives and Iron Blues to make an appearance. Sedges will be flying over the water and there may be enough of them to bring an odd trout splashing up to the surface.

Strange things may happen in summer. In August, ants may suddenly descend on the water and the trout may wake up to feed on them steadily. Artificial Red Ants are worth their place in a fly-box. Then, in the shade of a tree, a big trout may be waiting to feed on land-flies or bugs or beetles, or anything that drops from the leaves and branches. It is worth watching the water under trees carefully. These trout may not rise every minute, or even every five minutes, but they are frequently there and ready to be caught.

Spinners may visit the stream to lay their eggs at any time on a summer's day. But for most of it there may be little fly. Unless you are on a chalk-stream you will 'fish the water' rather than 'fish the rise'. The trout have changed their positions since Spring. Rain-fed rivers look rather different now that the water-level has dropped. The deep, quiet pools still hold trout but they are mostly lazy, disinterested fish, since the water there tends to be staler and worse-oxygenated than in the faster shallows. The hungrier, more energetic fish will be in the shallow runs, or in the stickles, where the rippling water mixes with the air and absorbs some of its oxygen. In the evenings trout may rise all over the river.

In the still water of lakes and reservoirs, however, trout will forsake the shallows on hot days. They will seek really deep water—twenty feet down or over—because there, below the 'thermocline', the water-temperature is cooler. Until the evening, reservoir fishermen may not succeed with a dry fly.

Chalk-stream fishermen are much more fortunate in high summer than most. Olives, Iron Blues and Pale Wateries continue to hatch, somewhat spasmodically but not too badly. These chalk-streams are spring-fed—they come welling up cool and clear from the chalk—and the level of them alters very little. The chalk downs act as a perpetual reservoir. The rivers may rise or fall a little but not nearly so much as the rain-fed streams. This means that floods and droughts are virtually unheard of. The temperature is more constant too. That is why water-cress, which flourishes in an even temperature, grows so well in Hampshire. Both trout and flies find the even temperature to their liking, so that although the days of July and August may be poor compared with those of earlier months, a chalk-stream fisherman can usually bargain on coming across feeding trout.

What can you reasonably expect from a good summer's day on a chalk-stream? A great deal of fun. There is not only a chance of having one or two fish in the bag; there is also an immense variety in the number of different problems you meet during the day. The trout will seldom rise so well as they did in Spring but they will rise for a longer time each day and behave in more interesting ways. One of the charms of summer fishing is that every success is a small triumph. Earlier on you are really supposed to catch fish. You yourself imagine that you will, and all your friends imagine that you will. Your wife imagines that you will, too. If you come home without at least two brace you may even put out the housekeeping. But now if you bring home one brace you feel a hero.

During the comparatively brief hatches of April it is practically impossible not to be keyed-up and a little nervous. In April, if you have no luck by the time the fly dwindles away, you become angry with yourself because you know you have missed your opportunities for the whole day. You incline to dash from one fish to the next. In July, however—when trout may be on the feed for longer hours—fishing can be less hurried. If you see a trout rising, you can take your time to approach him and to study his habits. If he defeats you, you can afford to look for another trout without haste, and if that one happens to defeat you as well you can always pin your hopes on a truly splendid evening rise.

Suppose, for instance, you arrive on the water about ten-thirty one morning? If you care to drag yourself out of bed you can of course arrive earlier, and you may find hatches of *Caenis* —or Fisherman's Curse—on the slower and siltier stretches of water shortly after dawn. *Caenis* is the smallest member of the Ephemeropteran group of flies. A tiny stubby-winged insect, it may hatch out at any time from the end of May onwards and, as its nickname implies, it is no great help to a fisherman. Trout may possibly fall to a Caenis or Last Hope or Lunn's Yellow Boy when they are feeding on *Caenis* but often they ignore every artificial fly completely.

Ten-thirty is perhaps rather soon for there to be much other activity, but I do not think any fisherman ever regrets getting to his water with time to spare. Nothing is more upsetting than to arrive half-way through a rise, since then if you do not catch anything you have only yourself to blame for being so late. If you come early, before life on the river has really begun to move, this moment of arrival can be wonderfully pleasant. You make your way through the woods or through the meadows till quite suddenly you come upon the stream. There it is, your hunting ground for the whole day. You can hardly help being optimistic as you set up your rod in peace, sit down to await events and think to yourself: 'When the first trout rises, I expect he'll rise *there*'.

Another reward of arriving early is that although you may be very busy later in the day, now you can take time off to watch things going on all round. You can keep a solicitous eye on your favourite family of duck, as they swim in and out of the reeds, with the mother in the lead and children paddling themselves busily along behind her. Why is there always one ridiculous duckling who lags two or three yards behind all the rest and causes such tremendous trouble? Your day may be made by the rare flash of a kingfisher. Young pheasants, young moorhens (I don't like coots), young plovers and redshanks—all these will be about. And plenty of other birds and animals, including the water-rat. Or the water-vole, to give him his correct name. No river-scene is complete without an officious water-vole swimming from bank to bank, occasionally sitting up on a raft of weed to eat a reed-stem in his hands, just like a child eating a banana.

The river valley will have a sleepy beauty by now. The lushness of the greens can become almost monotonous—but often the green of the cornfields is colourfully relieved by the red of poppies, the white of campion, or the yellow of mustard. In the water-meadows themselves there should be rosebay willowherb, meadow-sweet, yellow flag, purple loosestrife, forget-me-nots and enough other plants to make a brave show.

Today, while you are waiting and watching and before any flies hatch, you see a trout start to feed on nymphs. At your feet is a green bed of ranunculus and by its side a golden patch of gravel. Suddenly a trout sidles out of the weed, lies on the gravel for a minute or two and then moves slowly upstream. Shortly afterwards there is a swirl on the surface, and after that another swirl several yards beyond, showing that the trout is taking nymphs on his way.

You consider trying to catch this trout on a nymph. Eventually you decide against the plan. It is always difficult to cast precisely for moving fish and all too often they play follow-my-leader with you. You may rush up-stream, casting every few yards, until they deceive you utterly by stopping still for a little so that you over-run them and put them down. Worse still, you may disturb several other fish. So you let this trout be. Early in the day it often does far more harm than good to charge up and down the river-bank before trout have started to feed properly. Patience may be a virtue here—though, contrary to popular belief, you seldom need much patience for dry-fly fishing. It is far too nerve-racking. Think of all the full-grown twelve-stone men you find shivering and quaking with fear behind a bush in case a half-pound trout should see them.

When you have waited another half-hour or so, a few Pale Wateries begin to hatch and the trout are not slow to take advantage of them. You try to choose a sizeable fish out of several who have now started to rise in full view. There is, after all, no sense at all in catching under-sized fish just for the sake of it—even though you may intend to return them to the water. Some may be so badly hooked that they have to be killed. And sometimes even lightly-hooked fish can be mortally damaged, particularly if the hook has caught hold in the tongue or gills. They may swim away and die later.

Two good trout are rising in mid-stream. You can guess they are large because they rise stolidly, confidently, without any of the splash that a small trout often makes when he comes up for a dun. They seem to displace a fair amount of water. Occasionally you catch a sight of their big, black nebs, which is a sure sign that they are not taking nymphs. The upper of the two fish looks slightly better, but if you cast for him first you will certainly put down the other. So you decide to start by attacking the lower one and hope to catch the pair of them.

At the third or fourth cast your Tups Indespensable lands in the right place. The trout surges up to it and you strike. There is a brief feeling of resistance, then a sickening slackness, and you see a turmoil in the water as the trout goes off to the dentist. Did you strike too soon? Did you pull the fly out of his jaws before he closed them and turned down? That seems the most likely answer. You determine not to make the same mistake twice, as you wait for the second of the two trout to show himself once more before you cast.

But, unfortunately, the second trout fails to rise again. The little flurry of Pale Watery has died away. Now the sun, coming out from behind a cloud, shines down upon a river that has suddenly become lifeless. It was a very short hatch. One or two young fish flop up spasmodically but they are too small and they are not rising steadily. You walk upstream and have a look round the next bend. Sure enough, there is a trout rising quietly in by the bank. The Tups Indispensable goes over him. He pays no attention to it.

You watch the trout for a little. Just because the Tup succeeded once, you cannot by any means guarantee that it will do so again. In summer there are so many different flies on the water throughout the day that two trout next door to each other may even be feeding on completely separate varieties. They may also change their diet from hour to hour, so that the only true guide is the evidence of the fisherman's own eyes at the time.

As you watch him the trout rises very gently, sipping down something that you cannot see. It might be spinner. Since you have noticed an occasional Olive Spinner on the water, you take a Lunn's Particular from your box and try it on the fish. This time there is no bungling. The trout takes it firmly and is well hooked. Then you realize, to your disappointment, that he is undersized after all. The trouble is that when trout rise to spinners a four-pounder may make just as tiny a dimple as a quarter-pound baby.

You guide the little fish to where you are standing, then you slide your fingers down the cast till they grasp the shank of the hook, and you wiggle it about in the water. The trout kicks off and swims away happily, never having left his native element. This is a good way of returning trout provided they are not severely hooked.

Just upstream are some shallows, where you think you may find a fish. There does not seem to be very much happening but you can clearly see one medium-sized trout hovering over a patch of gravel between two weed-beds, obviously on the look-out for fly. He rises once almost immediately, making a scarcely discernible break in the rough water. Several Medium Olives are hatching so you tie on a Hare's Ear and offer it to the trout. He takes it—you strike—the hook goes home—and the fish dashes downstream to bury himself in a dense clump of weed at your feet. (Many fish work their way a few yards upstream from their homes to feed, and when they are hooked their first thought is 'Home, James', so they usually make their first run downstream.) You try hand-lining this trout and it works. He comes clear of the weeds and after a little more excitement you land your first sizeable fish of the day.

He weighs about a pound and a quarter. As you continue upstream afterwards you nearly walk on top of another trout. You suddenly catch sight of his tail. The tail is sticking out from under a patch of floating weed. As you watch you can see the trout move out into the stream and almost immediately move back to his hiding-place under the weed. Here is a trout who is lying in shelter but also keeping an eye out for passing nymphs or shrimps. Perhaps a Pheasant Tail nymph, passing down by the side of the weed-bed, might tempt him?

You make a cast—either a good one or a lucky one. Out comes the trout. You tighten—and yes, you have him on. Thank goodness, he makes for the open water and three minutes later one more sizeable fish is on the bank. This trout was an unexpected catch, and you might easily never have noticed him. During the summer, when there are no big hatches of fly, it is well worth-while scanning every bit of the riverbed that you can see. You may find trout who can be induced to feed. A motionless trout glued to the bottom will seldom take anything, but a trout that appears alive and active—especially if he is poised in mid-water or near the surface—may grab a sunk nymph or come up for a floating fly. A big sedge or Caperer sometimes does the job. The important thing, of course, is to see these trout before you are so close to them that they take fright.

By now it is two o'clock. Two sizeable fish, one undersized fish, and one fish pricked. Not too bad. While you are wondering whether any more fresh fly will hatch it starts to rain and a few duns re-appear on the water. The trout start rising again. This time the rise lasts a little longer and there are Medium Olives on the water for about three-quarters of an hour. During this hatch you lose one trout and catch another sizeable one, only just over a pound but a nice plump fish. Also you miss a couple of fish. When the rise finally peters out you are left with a feeling that you might have done a little better.

A hundred yards further on, a trout is steadily sip-sip-sipping under an old tree overhanging some smooth water. The sky has now cleared and as the trout moves into a shaft of sunlight you can see his black shape. He is undoubtedly a big trout. Perhaps he is taking spinner? There do not seem to be any spinner on the water but you try the trout with a Houghton Ruby, a Pheasant Tail and a Tup. None of them interest him at all so you decide that he must be feeding on smut and that a Black Gnat may catch him.

You show him a tiny Black Gnat and a little hump appears on the surface near your fly as the trout comes up to inspect it, then refuses it and goes down again. That was a close shave. You present the Black Gnat to him a second time but he takes no more notice of it, nor can he be attracted by any of your other small flies. He goes on rising persistently. In desperation you knot on a large Caperer. Almost before it reaches him he dashes at it like a tiger. In great surprise and completely off your guard, you strike badly, prick him hard and see him flounder on the top of the water for a couple of seconds before the hook loses its hold. A shame. Despite the difference in size, smutting trout do sometimes take Caperers very readily. Perhaps the juicy bulk of these large flies makes them look good mouthfuls to a trout working hard at small insects.

As you walk back downstream you see a trout's tail waving like a banner above the surface of the river. The trout has his nose buried deep in some weed and is literally standing on his head as he searches for shrimp. You put a Pope's Nondescript over him, choosing one of the intervals when he takes his head out of the weed. A Pope's Nondescript, says Skues, will occasionally catch a tailing trout. This does not seem to be one of the occasions. The trout never even looks at your fly so you leave him to his acrobatics and continue downstream.

The river looks fairly dead now. Flies and fish are both taking a rest. But at about four-thirty some spinners begin coming down on the water. You can see them as they are carried along by the quiet current, and their red bodies and white wings show that they are Iron Blue spinners. So onto the end of your cast goes a Houghton Ruby. Meanwhile, a fish has started to rise every twenty seconds or so under the far bank. Your Houghton Ruby drops over there. Another rise and you strike. This time a rather larger trout forges upsteam, playing deep and heavy, so that you have to follow him.

After two minutes of playing you still have not caught a glimpse of your trout. You think he must be big. He is not taking out much line but when he does he takes it out without any effort at all and he feels really solid. He might be any size. After another minute he comes in under your own bank and you see him to be a thick fish of at least two pounds. He sees you at the same time, which sends him off on another headlong tour of the stream. Will you never land him? He tires slowly, and then you slide the net under him, praying fervently that you will not lose him at the last moment as he thrashes around on the surface. All goes well, luckily, and eventually you hang him on your spring-balance to find you have landed a fish of two and a quarter pounds—a big trout by any standard.

While the spinners are still falling you catch another under-sized trout. This one, unfortunately, is not nearly so lightly hooked as the first one and you cannot release him without lifting him onto the bank. Here is the way you do it. Before handling him at all you wet your hands carefully so as not to rub off any of the slime that protects his skin. Then, when he is on the bank, you try to ease the hook out tenderly to avoid tearing his mouth. The process takes quite a little while and when you replace him in the water he starts to turn belly-upwards. If the stream carries him away in such a state he may get into trouble, so you hold him in the water with his head upstream till he regains his breath, wriggles out of your hand and goes off to recuperate in a weed-bed.

By the time you have finished doing this it is nearly six o'clock and the spinner-rise is over. The stream will probably stay quiet now until the evening rise starts. You can go home with a clear conscience to have some supper before coming back to fish again an hour or so before sunset. As for lunch, you have probably taken the opportunity of a lull in the fishing to eat some sandwiches—if you remembered them. Pocketable sandwiches are a great blessing to fishermen. Set meals are a great curse. If you are expected back at your host's house or any other meeting-place for a cooked lunch you can be quite certain the trout will begin rising at that very hour. Good hosts and good landlords have usually learned through bitter experience that fishing guests are rather erratic time-keepers.

Today has been a very good day, with its five sizeable fish. It has not, however, been quite exceptional. There has been great variety in it and continual hope all day long. I myself do rather like to catch trout when I go fishing. (One looks such an idiot if one doesn't.) But even if I only catch one sizeable fish on a summer's day I am always very glad that I did not stay at home to wait for the evening rise.

Chapter 12

The End of it All

September is a good month for fishermen, albeit a sad one in ways. The days are much shorter now, and the thought that autumn is waiting impatiently to blow the green leaves away makes every hour more precious. The season is drawing to its close, but gloriously so. The fields have turned from green to gold, and although the noon sun seems almost as warm as ever, it is no longer the thick, sultry heat of August. Wispy mists cover the countryside in the early morning, and on the way to the river, the sun shimmers through myriads of starry, dewy spider-threads strung from leaf to leaf and reed to reed. And, if the spiders are busy and active during September, the trout are often no less so.

While fishermen make the most of their last few weeks of the season, the trout may be equally keen to make the most of good feeding before they start to spawn. Then they will feed very little. As soon as their spawning activities begin, food ceases to interest them so much. In any case there is not nearly so much food to be had in the winter months. So while the food is available, and while they are hungry, they feed well.

September, whatever the weather, is nearly always better than August. Fishing may begin to pick up in the last week of August, if plenty of Black Gnats appear on the water. Black Gnats are rather uncertain creatures. Unlike Olives and Iron Blues, which hatch in fair numbers every year, Black Gnats may arrive in millions one year, to be practically absent the next. May is a good month for them. After that there are very few to be seen till about August 20th. Then for a fortnight, the Black Gnat season can occasionally provide really splendid fishing, with as many fish rising as during the Mayfly.

This may only happen in one year out of many. But that year is worth waiting for. The common Black Gnat—a *Bibio* type—hatches on land and lays its eggs on land. It is not really a water-fly at all, and you do not have a proper 'hatch' of Black Gnats. It only falls on the water by mistake, or when it is dead. So there has to be a tremendous quantity of Black Gnats about, before enough can fall on the river to bring the trout up. And, in a good year for Black Gnats, there are swarms of them about. They cover the plants by the side of the water, particularly all the white 'umbrella' plants. Whenever you notice that these plants are hardly white any longer, but almost black with the tiny insects, you can bank on a very good day's fishing.

The day may start in a normal way, with a few trout feeding on Pale Wateries or Medium Olives, or on their spinners. Then the Black Gnats will begin to fall. The important thing here is to change to a Black Gnat quickly, however keen fish may have seemed to take other flies beforehand. While they are feeding on Black Gnats they will seldom take anything else. The insects on the plants will have provided some warning of what to expect, and the Black Gnats themselves are quite easy to see on the smoother parts of the stream. They look like small, dark-coloured bundles. As they are usually dead or dying, and cannot escape, the trout take them steadily and quietly, without any fuss at all.

Falls of Black Gnat are seldom continuous throughout the day. They may commence at any time from eleven o'clock onwards. After a fall there may be a lull, when only an occasional Black Gnat floats down, and then a little later the surface will again be speckled with them. They often float downstream in clusters. During the lulls, the trout may revert to other flies, or stop rising until the next fall. The trout always seem to love Black Gnats, provided there are plenty of them, and the falls may go on intermittently until three or four o'clock.

Most stretches of water have one or two dead bits where hardly any trout ever seem to rise. This is often because the river-bed has become silted-up there, and very few flies like it. But Black Gnats are an exception. They drop down more or less at random all over the valley, and as many will drop on the poor bits of the river as on the better fly-bearing bits.

So if the Black Gnats appear in strength, it is often worth visiting dead water, which will probably have been fished very little indeed. You may easily pick up a big old bottom-feeding trout, who would not dream of letting you find him on the surface at any time other than this, and perhaps in the Mayfly season.

A tying of a double Black Gnat, which is an imitation of two flies mating, can be very useful sometimes. The insects often sink down onto the water while paired together. The Black Gnats last well into September, and trout can sometimes be caught on them half-way through the month. Then, as soon as they die away, the other flies begin to hatch more regularly than they did in the heat of summer. The September hatches may make the season end with a bang, not a whimper. Pale Wateries will still be there, and more Medium Olives will hatch as the weather grows cooler. Towards the end of the month, a few Large Dark Olives may appear on the water again, for the first time since Spring. In October these flies hatch nearly every day, and they carry on throughout the winter, which means that although the fisherman only sees them for a brief period at the beginning and end of his season, they are really one of the commonest flies on most rivers.

Spinners, too, will be in evidence throughout the day and especially in the early evening. These September days are comparatively short, and all the more active because of it. There is no long lull between the daytime rise and the evening rise, as there is in July. Sometimes the two rises almost dovetail into each other, with scarcely a pause, so that you can fish solidly all day. You can have supper at a respectable hour too—after having fished the evening rise.

The trout in the river will be in good condition and they may even be ripe. When you clean them, you may find them heavy with milt or large eggs. But trout may not be the only fish in the water. There may be grayling as well. These, with their big dorsal fins, will be very fit now. You can look upon the silver grayling as either a game fish or a coarse fish, according to the way you feel about him. Grayling have big scales like many coarse fish. Their lips look better for sucking up food from the bottom than for feeding like a trout. Yet they take flies on the surface readily. They have none of the trout's colouring, but their adipose fins show that they originally came from the same family as trout and salmon. The adipose fin is the tiny, stumpy, useless fin between the big dorsal fin and the tail fin. It is supposed to be a remnant of the far-off days when all fish had one huge fin running the whole length of their backs. All the members of the salmon family have hung onto this last vestige of it.

Grayling, like coarse fish and unlike trout, spawn in the Spring. If you have any grayling in your river, you see them cavorting about on their spawning grounds as you are beginning your season's trout-fishing. You do not catch many of them then, because they take little interest in food while they are spawning. One or two, however, usually the small ones who have not yet begun to spawn, will always rise. The others wait till mid-May or June, and then begin to show themselves properly. On some rivers, where conditions suit them well, grayling are the fly-fisherman's chief quarry and they have ther own legal season from June 16th till March 14th. They were first introduced to the chalk-streams some time ago to provide fly-fishing during the Autumn for people who hated to put their rods away at the end of September. Unfortunately, however, they multiplied too fast for anyone's liking and now they are treated there as vermin—because they eat up the trout's food. To protect the trout, water-keepers and fishermen catch, net, electrocute and hunt the unfortunate grayling all the year round.

No-one can be blamed for doing this in an effort to improve expensive trout waters. But even so, I regard the grayling as a game fish. Admittedly, it is disappointing to catch a grayling when you expect a trout, but the grayling has much to be said in his favour. His chief virtue is that he rises freely and constantly. In the sweltering heat of a summer or early September afternoon, when too few flies are on the water to attract the lazy trout, grayling are nearly always prepared to rise. Whatever the flies may be, smuts or duns or spinners, they seem to whet a grayling's appetite.

Grayling do not rise in quite the same way as trout. Whereas a feeding trout likes to lie just below the surface, so that he can tilt up to take a fly with the minimum of effort, a grayling soars up to grab flies from a much deeper level, often from the river-bed itself. They are far quicker than trout and can often beat trout to a fly. Just as a trout is preparing to take a fly, in his own steady way, you may see a grayling dash up from below to steal it from him.

Another result of the grayling's swiftness is that he is very difficult to hook when you strike. First, he sometimes misses the fly in his haste. Second, if the fisherman strikes with the usual deliberation that he finds necessary for trout, he is often too late for grayling. I have seen many expert fishermen, who would scarcely ever fail to hook a trout, having their confidence in striking torn into shreds by missing grayling after grayling. I think one inevitably misses a great many grayling, the only saving feature being that one usually has another chance at them. They are less easily put off the rise than trout, and after a grayling has been missed, he may easily rise again to the same fly three or four times, until you eventually succeed in hooking him.

When trout are rising and when trout are needed for the pot more than grayling, it is useful to be able to distinguish between the rises of the two fish. Unfortunately mistakes are only too common. If, however, several fish are all rising together in a small area, they are more likely to be grayling than trout, because grayling live in shoals while trout never do. If you catch sight of a tail above the water as the fish dives down, particularly a forked tail, it will probably be a grayling-rise, since grayling have forked tails which often break the surface as they turn sharply downwards. Grayling, on the whole, rise more splashily than trout. And they are less shy about rising in the open, in fact they seem to prefer it. A fish feeding under a bank, therefore, or right up against a weed-bed, is liable to be a trout.

When there is very little fly, and hardly a trout rising, the grayling can provide excellent substitute sport. And when the trout season is over, grayling fishing is by any standard a fine sport in its own right. It takes an arrant snob with quite the wrong values to disdain grayling fishing, and I am sorry for fishermen who do. Grayling make good eating, too. If you scale them—or better still, skin them—they will be all the tastier. It is one of the great advantages of flyfishing that the old epithet 'the unspeakable in pursuit of the uneatable' cannot be applied to it.

Grayling like much the same flies as do trout, though they are probably not so discriminating. They can always be caught on an imitation of the fly that is hatching. But they can also be lured by a flash of colour, and a bright fly like a Red Tag is very successful for them. Sometimes big bags of them are caught in the chalk-streams on a wet fly, usually in late Autumn when the trout season is over, and when the weeds have died down to let the wet fly be fished easily. Grayling can grow fairly heavy. Two-pounders are not rare on the chalk-streams. A normal adult grayling is about the same size as an adult trout. The record grayling, however, stands at only seven pounds and two ounces. Grayling differ from their cousins in that they seldom feed on the smaller fish that go to nourish great trout.

One thought that may (and should) pass through the fisherman's mind in September is water-improvement. What can be done to make the fishing better before next April? In good trout waters with natural spawning grounds—always provided the waters have not been over-fished—the trout should be able to look after themselves. After all, they have done so for thousands of years. But very many waters nowadays *are* fished more heavily than is good for them, and you cannot take out hundreds of trout every year without giving the fish-population a helping hand to restore the balance.

Should you, for instance, stock with young trout? And if so, how young should they be? A sizeable trout, reared to maturity, is more likely to survive when he is put into the river than a younger one, but then he is more expensive to buy. It costs at least a pound today to buy three of them. At the other end of the scale, it is possible to stock with trout-eggs or fry, provided suitable nurseries have been prepared in the water. Ideally, these should be clean, gravelly side-streams carefully protected by grids and wire from birds, pike and other trout-enemies. The young trout can be released into the main river when they are old enough to look after themselves properly. This is a cheap way of stocking, but many of the eggs and the young trout will die. Between these two extremes, stocking can be carried out with yearlings or two-year-olds.

But none of these stocked trout, at whatever age they are introduced, will live and grow unless conditions in the river or lake are first made right for them. If there is too little oxygen or if there are too few good lies, they will die or go elsewhere if they can. If there is too little food, the big fish will become lanky, while the small trout will either starve or remain as dwarfs. Again, if the water is infested by pike or coarse fish, the trout stand little chance.

Once the water is put right, your trout will thrive, and you may even be able to give up the idea of stocking altogether. With the right conditions, Nature herself provides the best and cheapest way of producing trout, and will produce as many as the food in the river will support. Of course, where no spawning-beds exist, or where the water is so feequently fished that too few trout are left at the season's end to make up for the season's losses, owners have no choice and are forced to stock every year. Reservoirs, too, usually have inadequate spawning grounds and rely on the 'put and take' form of fishing—that is, you get out what you put in. Or to be more precise, you get out at least a percentage of what you put in.

Regular stocking is an essential policy for many a good fishery. And after a few weeks in the water, stocked trout will become as shy and difficult to catch as wild ones. Nevertheless, there are many fishermen who would rather catch a half-pound wild trout than a three-pound rainbow who started life in a trout-farm. Both sorts of trout have their place in the scheme of things, and we should not disparage either of them.

Food, oxygen, good lies, clean spawning-beds, these are the important things. And freedom from enemies, too. So as a fisherman works his way upstream at the end of the season, he will probably cast a critical eye over his water, his mind busy with plans. Those shallows above the wood, for instance— the trout will be spawning there soon. If they were raked, and the gravel loosened, the trout-eggs would have a better chance of safe cover between the stones. Here is one job to be done without delay. Then how about those other shallows, where there is even less depth of water, where the stream rushes and bubbles and gurgles so hastily that few trout can lie there without having to fight the current? Can anything be done? A few boulders, scattered over the shallows, would at least provide shelter for one or two trout and insects. Or better still, a dam or groyne just downstream would raise the level of the water a few inches, hold it up, slow it down, allow weed to grow and trout to live above the obstruction.

Perhaps, again, the fisherman may pass by a slow, silted stretch of his water, half-choked by weed, some of it dying. He has caught very few fish in it this season. One or two trout do live there, but they do not rise and—yes, he can see a pike basking on the top of the water by the reeds. What should be done? The pike, of course, can be wired or electrocuted. If there are plenty of pike, they may even provide some good sport on rod and line during the winter.

But this is not getting to the root of the problem. The real trouble is that the current is too sluggish. It is not fast enough to carry particles of silt along so it deposits them. Even if all the mud were scooped out—which can be arranged, at some expense—exactly the same thing would happen later. The current would deposit more silt, clumps of still-water weed would begin to grow again, and the pike would re-establish themselves. No—either the amount of water must be increased, so that it flows faster, or the area over which it flows must be made smaller. The only way of obtaining more water, unfortunately, is to take it from somewhere else. Sometimes this is a practical possibility, when the river has a system of hatches leading to side-streams or carriers, but often it can be dangerous, since other parts of the river may suffer, or the whole irrigation system of the meadows be upset.

The second measure, however, is often feasible. It means, in effect, narrowing the river-bed. If hurdles, for instance, are staked into the river, jutting diagonally out from the bank, the current will flow faster as it goes round the hurdles. If each hurdle has a similar one opposite it on the far bank, the current will then be concentrated in the centre of the stream and will sweep the mud away. Silt will only be deposited in limited areas, in the slow water behind the hurdles. These deposits can be planted with sedges, and later with other vegetation, so that they become firm. Eventually the hurdles can be moved to do their work elsewhere, leaving behind them a stretch of water with a faster flow and a cleaner river-bed in the middle. Alternatively hurdle islands can be built in mid-stream, with the object of diverting and concentrating the flow on either side. Used properly, the current is by far the cheapest and best means of keeping the river free from too much silt.

Then, the fisherman will inspect his weeds closely—almost as lovingly as a gardener inspecting his flower-beds. Will there be enough water-plants next year to provide cover for trout and food for trout-food? He wants clean weed, growing on gravel if possible. Surveying the river bed, he can see plenty of starwort, with its starry clusters of tiny leaves. Ranunculus and water-celery are plainly in evidence, too. All these are good weeds, holding plenty of fly and shrimp. But there are some bad weeds about as well—mare's tail and long, wavy ribbon-weed. These are not nearly so hospitable to trout-food.

Should he try to root these bad weeds out? Perhaps so, if there are many of them. Mere cutting will be no long-term remedy. But if he uproots them, he may well be able to encourage more useful weeds to grow in their place, weeds that collect algae but not mud, weeds that will harbour thriving colonies of fly-larvae. Of these the starwort is probably the most adaptable. It will grow in quite fast water, and also in slow water. Its main trouble is that it does tend to collect silt. Where the current is fast enough to keep it clean and well oxygenated, it is a useful weed and will provide a home for many of the creatures that trout feed on. But where the current is slow—and particularly where it is slow and shallow—it will quickly become clogged with silt and may soon begin to choke the stream. A useful rule-of-thumb is to try to eliminate starwort where the water is less than eighteen inches deep, but to leave a fair growth of it elsewhere.

Rather better than the starwort are two weeds called ranunculus (or water buttercup) and water-celery. Small water-animals live in them readily, and they collect comparatively little silt. These weeds will not flourish in very deep or very sluggish water, but they grow well in most stretches of the chalk-streams. Usually, if other weeds are removed to make room for them, they will take root naturally. Or you can plant them by dropping them into the river with stones tied to their roots, heavy enough to keep them in place while they gain a hold on the river-bed. Or bunches of them, with their roots tied up in hessian bags, can be pushed into the silt or into holes dug in the gravel.

We all dream of perfect trout water. We shall love and cherish it, and we shall have the freedom of it. If it is a lake or reservoir, we may perhaps dream of beating the trout record every year. We can imagine ourselves, in a decade or two, feeling rather sorry for the members of the British Record (Rod-caught) Fish Committee. Every year they will have to mutter into their grey beards: 'Not Mr. . . . . *again!*'

If we enjoy rivers more, we may not be able to dream up visions of such large fish. But to compensate for this, our dreams will be in colour, the bright colours of green and gold. There will be the vivid green of healthy weed and the gold of clean gravel. The trout will be many, and fat, and free-rising, because the stream will be full of food for them. Our perfect water will be a paradise for trout and for ourselves.

We all carry these dreams in our minds, and we hug them to our hearts. The tragedy is that although we could often do so much towards bringing them to life on our own rivers, we seldom do quite enough. Frequently we try to have our cake and eat it. We catch trout, and still expect to find them there next week. Sometimes we fail to take proper care not to fish for undersized fish. Sometimes, during the Mayfly or on other duffers' days, we kill more fish than we have any right to expect. Again, when we realise perfectly well that a day or two spent with stakes and hurdles and spades, instead of fishing-rods, would repay us amply—we prefer to fish on.

But no-one can stop us dreaming. And as we walk up the riverbank in September, we rehearse all the thoughts and hopes that will support us through the coming close-season. We shall see those green banks from arm-chairs, from bus-queues and from office desks.

Meanwhile, however, the last evening of the last day has

arrived, and we are fishing the evening rise for the very last time. There has been plenty of fly, and we have done well, but now it is almost too dark to fish at all. One trout is still rising. He has refused us frequently already. Perhaps one last cast would catch him? No? Then, one more. No? Just a final one, then. No. A flight of ducks whistles overhead, and a breath of cold air rustles the reed-tops.

It is September 30th. The season is over.

PART FOUR

ODDS AND ENDS

APPENDIX A

Questions of Tackle

SECTION 1 RODS

SECTION 4 PRESENTATION, LEADERS AND SUNDRIES

Section 1

Rods

Rods will take up the major part of this appendix and it is only logical to begin with them. They are such an obvious choice to talk about first, as the most ostentatious and highly-prized items in the whole armoury of fishing, that a word or two needs to be said about their limitations. No rod, for instance, can ever make a bad fisherman cast well, let alone fish well.

A good rod, if it is carefully matched to other good equipment, will certainly allow a fisherman to cast as well as he can. But the matching is just as important as the rod itself. Useful though a good rod may be, it is only one link in a chain, one part in a succession of parts—beginning with the brain-cells that tell a fisherman's muscles what to do, and ending with the fly.

The proverbial chain is no stronger than its weakest link. And if any part of the casting chain is inferior or ill-matched, whether it be the fisherman's reflexes or the line, the most expensive rod in the world won't help. The most frequent example of this must be the use of lines that don't balance the rod. Countless fishermen get discouraged about their casting because they're using a line that's too heavy or too light. A good rod with the wrong line won't perform so well as a bad rod with the right line.

Still, all this having been said, there is no doubt that a good rod is a perfect joy. Good tackle does indeed start with a good rod. A rod may be only a tool—for the fisherman is always the master and his skill counts for more than any of his tackle—but it is an immensely satisfying tool. A well-made and well-used rod is something to treasure, something that evokes a great sense of pride.

Every rod, to a fisherman, is an individual thing. For although two rods may be exactly alike, no two fishermen are exactly alike. The same rod will perform a little differently for each of them. Different rods are made to suit different purposes and different physiques. I hope here to explain some of these differences.

There is one other aspect of rods that is worth mentioning. A fisherman can have a long and happy love-affair with a well-made rod, and so he should. Like a favourite and time-honoured tweed coat, a rod will take on part of his personality. They learn to get on well together. Even the most bad-tempered of fishermen can become sentimental over a rod.

But do we know our rods well enough? I have an uneasy feeling that some other countries can put us a little in the shade. In America, for instance, rods are a great talking-point among fishermen away from the river. They are continually brought out and shown off. They are carefully examined, enviously admired, testily criticised, hotly defended, fiercely disputed—and compared at length.

This is something I can't help liking. It is great fun, for one thing. And it accords to rods the attention and respect they deserve. After all, rods have been created and developed with much the same pride and care as pictures or pottery. And a rod, just like a painting, usually has an interesting history. If it belonged to a relative, or to a famous fisherman, it can have a truly fascinating history.

I have sometimes heard people say that they would like to discuss rods in more detail, but that they simply didn't know which details to discuss. No one had told them more than a few elementary facts about rods. It's surprising, but there is hardly any published information about them—or rather, about their finer points. Several up-to-date books exist on the making of guns, but hardly a single one on rods.

Yet a little knowledge about rods greatly increases the pleasure of owning one. If these few pages help anyone to take more pleasure in owning a rod, or to know what to look for when choosing and buying one, they will have been well worth writing.

Q.1.   WHAT MATERIALS CAN I CHOOSE FROM?

The three great rod-building materials are carbon fibre (called graphite in the U.S.A.), cane (called bamboo in the U.S.A.) and fibreglass, which thank goodness goes by the same name in both countries.

The order in which they're given above is their order of expense. A good carbon-fibre rod will be the most expensive and a good fibreglass rod the least expensive, while a good cane rod will come somewhere in between, probably closer to carbon fibre than to fibreglass.

No single one of these materials is necessarily 'better' for every-one than the other two. They all have advantages for different people and in different circumstances. So it's worth going into their characteristics at a little length, if only because it may save you from spending more money than you need.

Q.2.   WHAT ARE THE CHARACTERISTICS OF CARBON-FIBRE FLYRODS?

The material called carbon fibre was first invented in England for the aerospace industry, at the Royal Aircraft Establishment, Farnborough, in 1965. It was in America, however, that it was mainly developed for use in flyrods. Carbon-fibre flyrods became available in Britain in 1974/75, about a year later than in America. They very soon became popular. Why?

First of all, it's important to realise that there's no magic in carbon fibre. It won't suddenly turn a bad caster into a good one and it won't allow a beginner to learn how to cast overnight. The particular advantages of carbon fibre are relevant to a good many flyfishermen and a good many flyfishing situations – but by no means to all.

Second, there's no such thing as a truly 'typical' carbon-fibre rod. It can be a mistake, therefore, to expect that just because a rod is made of carbon fibre, it'll behave in a particular way. The actions of carbon-fibre rods do vary a lot with the way they're made – though they'll obviously have one or two properties in common. As with rods of any other material, there are good carbon-fibre rods and bad ones. Carbon-fibre rods can be butt-action or tip-action (see pages 172–180), over-stiff or over-floppy – or just right. Some may suit you, some almost certainly won't. Here are the main characteristics of carbon fibre:

(a) *Weight.* Carbon fibre is remarkably light for its strength. On average, a carbon-fibre flyrod should weigh 40% less than an equivalent cane flyrod, and 25% less than an equivalent glass flyrod. A certain amount depends on the weight of the reel-fitting and other furnishings, of course. A carbon-fibre rod should have light fittings. Ideally, it should also be used with a light reel.

In practice, the lightness of carbon fibre means that a caster has less weight to move. So he can cast a given distance with less force. *Or*, given the same force, he can cast a little further – usually a couple of yards or so. *Or* he can use a longer rod, without finding it too much effort. For instance, excellent stillwater and grilse rods of 10 or even 11 feet, weighing no more than 4 or 5 oz., are made possible by carbon fibre. But don't go to an extreme length – because a rod that's altogether too long will exert a lot of leverage on the wrist, however light it may be.

(b) *Diameter.* Because carbon fibre as a raw material is so strong, less of it is needed to make a flyrod. Carbon-fibre flyrods, therefore, have small diameters. They're beautifully slim. Compared with glass rods, they're particularly slim at the butt – and this helps them to have an 'all-through' action.

The slimness of carbon-fibre rods also means that they offer very little air-resistance. This isn't a petty matter either. It's another reason why carbon-fibre flyrods need less force to cast a given distance. You not only have less weight to move, but you also have less air-resistance to overcome while you're moving it. This factor is most noticeable casting into a wind.

(c) *Stiffness.* Carbon fibre is far stiffer as a raw material than cane or glass. But this doesn't mean that a carbon-fibre flyrod will necessarily be stiffer in action – because the inherent stiffness of the material is offset during manufacture by using smaller diameters (and sometimes by other means as well).

When you first pick up a carbon-fibre flyrod, it may *feel* rather stiff until you start using it with a line. But that's simply because the tip is so light. Unlike the tips of other rods, it won't 'swing' of its own accord. There's too little weight to make it swing. But as soon as you're casting with a line of the right weight, the rod will flex perfectly.

(d) *Speed.* Carbon fibre has a faster 'rate of recovery' than cane or glass. (That is to say, it takes less time to straighten from an induced bend.) But we must be careful here. The final flyrod can be made to be comparatively 'fast' or comparatively 'slow'.

So you needn't speed up your casting – give the rod time to do its work. Nevertheless, you'll usually find that a carbon-fibre rod is good at developing high line-velocity (for distance-casting) and good at throwing a tight loop (for into-the-wind casting). See page 174. But it won't do either without your help – you must be able to cast properly.

(e) *Versatility.* Carbon-fibre flyrods (partly because of their slimness and partly because they give a flyline so little weight and inertia to overcome) can be made for very light lines indeed. And they'll nearly always handle a wider range of line-weights than other rods can. (See page 197 for an explanation of the importance of line-weights.) Sometimes they'll operate quite satisfactorily with four or even five different line-weights. This may, for instance, save a reservoir fisherman from having to carry two rods –

one for distance-casting with a heavy line, another for more delicate fishing with a lighter line.

This doesn't mean, however, that there isn't an *optimum* line-weight for every rod and every purpose. There is. It only means that you can if you wish use heavier and lighter lines as well. Any sort of flyfishing rod – short or long – can be made successfully from carbon fibre.

(f) *Construction.* You've probably read a good many 'stories' implying that such-and-such a method of manufacture is the only good way of making carbon-fibre rods. Don't you believe it. Carbon fibre is a very versatile material and can be used in more than one way. There's nothing 'sacred', for instance, about any given proportion of carbon fibre in a flyrod.

All that matters is the performance of the final rod. And there's no single path that leads to this. It takes a variety of design skills and manufacturing skills. And here's another word of caution about construction. Carbon fibre is immensely strong as a raw material – but remember the small diameters of the finished rods. So don't treat a carbon-fibre rod as if it were unbreakable. It certainly won't be easily breakable – but give it the same care as you'd give any other rod. (One caution: don't use carbon fibre in places where either the rod or the line may touch power-cables.)

(g) *Is carbon fibre good value?* Only you can judge, in the light of your own needs. Carbon fibre is expensive. And for many people, probably most people, it isn't strictly necessary. It won't catch them any more trout. Fibreglass is an excellent rod-building material too – wonderfully efficient and very economical. And cane, besides being a superb material in its own right, also has a marvellous feel that's all its own – an easy 'forgiving' feel that many river-fishermen love.

If you're considering a carbon-fibre flyrod, one very important question to ask yourself is 'Will its particular advantages be of any use to me?' And another is 'Will it add to my pleasure?' And if the answer to either of these is No, you may be able to save yourself some money.

Q.3.   WHAT ARE THE CHARACTERISTICS OF CANE FLYRODS?

Many people love cane flyrods and the word 'love' is used advisedly. These rods are made of a *natural* material and need more hand-processes than any other sort of rod, the processes being carried out (normally) by a skilled and loving craftsman.

The 'split cane' or 'built cane' of which flyrods are made consists of six segments of *outer* cane (the hardest and strongest part of the original bamboo) carefully matched and put together to form a virtually *solid* rod. See A below. The fibreglass and carbon fibre of flyrods, on the other hand, are made into tubes. See B below.

Diagram 1

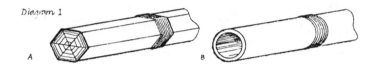

A   B

(a) *Weight.* Cane is the heaviest of the three materials. But in comparatively *short* rods this doesn't really matter at all, since the short length will make the rod delightfully light anyway. A carbon-fibre rod of 7 feet 6 inches should weigh only about 2 oz. But a cane rod of 7 feet 6 inches will still only weigh about 3½ oz., which is light enough for anyone.

Most people can handle a cane rod up to, say, 8 feet 9 inches with hardly any effort. But when it comes to rods which are 9 feet long or longer, lighter materials such as carbon fibre and glass do begin to have the advantage. I'd say that a rod of about 8 feet can easily be made of cane without becoming tiring, while a cane rod of 9 feet will be too heavy for most people. In between these two lengths you can choose whichever material suits your budget and gives you pleasure to use.

(b) *Diameter.* Because built cane is a more or less solid material a flyrod made of it can be comparatively slender, particularly at the butt, without running any risk of breaking. The diameter of a cane rod at the butt will probably not be quite so small as that of a carbon-fibre rod, but it will be a good deal smaller than that of a fibreglass rod.

This again helps the rod to have an 'all-through' action, working right down to your casting hand. An all-through action is a great advantage to accuracy. You feel you have complete control of the fly and that if you 'put your finger on the spot' the fly will go there too.

(c) *Stiffness.* One joy of cane (which it shares with carbon fibre) is that a cane rod can be as stiff or as flexible as the rod-designer chooses. It can be stiff and powerful if need be, or it can be flexible and delicate, helping your fly to alight on the water like thistledown. Cane lends itself particularly well to this latter type of rod.

Another advantage of cane's 'all-through' action is that it can cast equally well at a wide variety of distances. The fibres in cane stretch more easily than the fibres in glass (though not more easily than carbon fibres) so that a cane rod will work with very little line beyond the rod-tip. As line is lengthened the fibres continue to stretch and the rod continues to cast satisfactorily. By contrast, the fibres in most glass rods need more 'pull' from the line before they even begin to stretch. I'll describe the result in the answer to the next question, which is all about glass.

(d) *Speed.* To recapitulate, the 'speed' of a rod means the time it needs to straighten after an induced bend. This in turn depends upon the speed at which the fibres in a rod 'recover' their normal shape after stretching. Hence the phrase 'recovery rate' as an alternative to 'speed'.

Cane fibres stretch easily but 'recover' fairly slowly. This is a disadvantage when it comes to imparting high velocity to a line, which is essential for long-distance casting. But cane's leisurely action is a positive *advantage* for good 'presentation' – which means putting your fly down delicately on precisely the right square foot of water.

(e) *Versatility.* Cane rods are perhaps less versatile than rods made of other materials. For one thing, as I've mentioned above, they tend to feel a bit heavy if they're 9 feet or longer. This and their comparatively slow recovery rate make them less than ideal for long-distance casting, such as is often needed on large still waters. So on the whole they don't make good reservoir rods.

As against this they make superb river rods, provided the river doesn't need a rod longer than about 8 feet 6 inches or 8 feet 9 inches. They're not necessarily 'better' than carbon fibre, but they have a different feel – very deliberate and responsive. They can handle fairly light lines too. So the choice will be up to you.

(f) *Construction.* The details of a cane rod's construction are given under Q.16. It's worth observing that while carbon-fibre rods and fibreglass rods can be called miracles of science, only a hand-built cane rod deserves to be called a work of art.

(g) *Is cane good value?* If you fish large still waters, as I've explained already, a cane rod will be a hindrance. And it'll cost a good deal more than glass and almost as much as carbon fibre. But on medium-sized rivers and brooks, or wherever long-distance casting isn't a *sine qua non*, its flexibility and sensitivity can be a joy. It's not necessarily more efficient than carbon fibre, though it's usually a little superior to glass, neither is it less efficient. It's almost always a question of how much you like the unique 'feel' of cane, and then of how much you're prepared to pay for a rod you can 'love'.

Q.4. WHAT ARE THE CHARACTERISTICS OF FIBREGLASS FLYRODS?

Now we come to the least expensive of all rod-building materials, and the most popular. More glass rods are probably being used today than are cane and carbon-fibre rods put together. Glass rods wouldn't be so widespread if they were all 'cheap and nasty'. Many of them are cheap and *very* good for their purposes.

In fact this is as good as place as any to say that many of the differences I've pointed out, between one rod material and others, are fairly marginal. They're worth knowing about, so that if you wish you can get an ideal rod for the job you want it to do. But never forget that a good fisherman with a less-than-ideal rod will catch more fish than a less-good fisherman with an ideal rod. A vast quantity of fish are caught on glass flyrods.

(a) *Weight*. Glass comes between carbon fibre and cane. It's heavier than carbon fibre but lighter than cane – sufficiently so to allow, say, a glass rod of 9 feet 6 inches to be wielded by an ordinary man without too much effort. Equally, a glass rod of about 8 feet 6 inches makes an excellent first rod for an 8-year-old boy fishing a medium-sized stream.

Just a word about children. It's a mistake to give them too short a rod, however light it may be, because they'll find it all the more difficult to keep their back-casts up in the air. Also there won't be 'enough rod' to flex easily and to do the work *for* them. So give them an adult rod (about 8 feet 6 inches) which is also *light*. Fibreglass supplies enough lightness. And it's also inexpensive, an asset which will commend it to parents.

(b) *Diameter*. The tips of fibreglass rods can be fairly slim but for technical reasons the butts must be made rather thick if breakage is to be avoided. So a glass rod has a characteristically fat butt, a good deal fatter than those of equivalent rods made from other materials. This is one quick way of telling a glass rod from a carbon-fibre rod if the colour happens to be the same. (Carbon-fibre rods are usually black, while glass rods are usually – though not always – some shade of brown.)

As I've already mentioned (see page 144) glass rods are tubular. And any tube, if it's bent, is in some danger of becoming oval or elliptical where it's under greatest stress. See what happens when you bend a rolled-up newspaper. If this happened to a rod, in however small a degree, it would ruin the action. Careful attention to diameters and wall-thicknesses, as well as having the best material of its type, avoids any such defect in all *good* modern tubular rods.

(c) *Stiffness*. A glass rod can be made either stiff or supple for most of its length, but its fattish butt nearly always makes it rather stiff at that point. This means that if you want a supple glass rod you can get one – but you probably won't feel the action right down 'into the hand'. It's difficult, in fact, for such a rod to have a true 'all-through' action.

Fibreglass is therefore probably best suited to rods which are *comparatively* stiff throughout, as are all rods intended for fairly heavy lines. It is far easier then for the butt to make a worthwhile contribution to the rod's action and power.

(d) *Speed.* Glass is a 'faster' material than cane, though not so fast as carbon fibre. As with carbon fibre, however, a finished glass rod can be made with a 'slow action' or a 'fast action'. But in the former case there may be some difference between the speed of the butt and the speed of the rest of the rod.

This disparity, among other reasons, can lead a bad glass rod to 'bounce' at the end of the back-cast. Any 'bouncing' tendency will put waves into the aerialised part of the line, which then won't fall straight on the water. Good glass rods, needless to say, are free of this fault.

A glass rod with a fast action, like a carbon-fibre rod with a fast action, is an excellent tool for developing high line-velocity, and thus for casting a long way. It is also good for casting a tight loop (see page 174) and this makes it cast well into a wind.

(e) *Versatility.* Although glass is not so light as carbon fibre, it is probably best suited to rods intended to combine length with a good deal of lightness. Thus a glass rod is excellent for most forms of stillwater flyfishing. For fishing from the bank you'll need the capacity to throw a long line and a stiff-ish, powerful glass rod of about 9 feet 6 inches, used with a fairly heavy line, makes an admirable partnership.

For fishing still water from a boat a long rod is also useful, since it helps you to protract each retrieve and to bring the top fly of your team skittering across the water towards you. This is a time when trout often take it. For rods under 9 feet, especially if they're intended for light delicate lines, glass isn't perhaps *ideal*, but it can still be very serviceable.

(f) *Construction*. One of the most important aspects of constructing a glass tubular rod lies in the exact thickness of the 'walls' of the tube. It it's too thick the rod will be unnecessarily heavy and stiff. If it's too thin the rod will be very light, but it may break. This used to be a danger when manufacturers were all competing to see who could build the lightest glass rods, but it no longer happens with reputable makers. A good modern glass rod is very durable indeed.

   Fuller accounts of the construction of both cane and glass rods are given on pages 164 and 169.

(g) *Is glass good value?* By any standard, glass rods are very good value indeed. From a perfectionist's viewpoint, it's possible to argue that they aren't 'ideal'. A cane or carbon-fibre rod may be a little better for fishing delicately with a light line on brooks and streams. And a powerful carbon-fibre rod may be marginally better for casting long distances on still water. But in both instances glass won't be far behind – and not all of us can afford to fish exclusively with cane and carbon fibre.

Q.5. I'VE HEARD OF A NEW ROD MATERIAL CALLED 'BORON'. HOW ABOUT IT?

The following facts come from seeking very expert scientific advice and from testing a wide variety of carbon/boron rods. As a result I'm very sure that a proportion of boron in a flyrod doesn't automatically make it either *better or worse*.

Boron isn't actually so 'new' as carbon fibre. It was in fact invented some two years *before* carbon fibre. At one time it was developed for the aerospace industry but was then superseded by carbon fibre, which was more versatile and more easily workable. This was obviously a considerable blow to the manufacturers of boron, who then had to find other outlets for their production – such as the sporting-goods market.

For technical reasons a tubular 'boron' or 'carbon/boron' rod is unlikely to contain more than 15% to 20% boron – otherwise it would be too stiff. So, at any rate at the moment, any tubular rod which is advertised as 'boron' is actually made mainly of carbon fibre, with a smaller proportion of boron. A few experiments have been made in constructing rods of *solid* carbon fibre and solid boron, but it is too early to be sure where these will lead.

As a material boron is even stiffer than carbon fibre (55 mil. p.s.i. as opposed to 35 mil. p.s.i.). This allows a rod to be very slightly smaller in diameter. But it will not be any lighter – because boron is also some 50% heavier than carbon fibre (a 2.63 specific gravity, as opposed to 1.8).

A boron fibre cannot be bent so far as carbon fibre before it snaps. (It is a fatter fibre and has a larger 'minimum bend radius'.) This should not usually lead to fragility, except in certain situations such as when a fly is snagged in a tree and the rod-tip is given a sharp tug to free it. To offset this, boron is marginally better than carbon fibre at withstanding sudden knocks or impact, such as when a rod is dropped on to concrete. (Few enough rods, I hope, are subjected to either form of mistreatment.)

All these potential advantages and disadvantages are marginal, and they all cancel each other out. That's why I believe (and have found) that boron neither adds to nor detracts from a rod. A boron or carbon-fibre or carbon/boron rod should be judged on its action and performance, rather than on whether or not it contains boron.

Q.6   ARE ANY OTHER 'REVOLUTIONARY' NEW MATERIALS LIKELY TO COME ALONG?

It's possible. (A new material called Kevlar has already been added to a very few carbon-fibre rods in the States, but has not had any acclaim.) Unfortunately it's not unlikely that some new 'miracle' materials may be incorporated in rods mainly because of their advertising value, to imply that the rods are ultra-modern, rather than for any extra efficiency they may give the rod.

The use of carbon fibre in flyfishing rods was indeed a revolutionary step. But there seems to be no other material in the offing which is capable of making such a significant advance.

Q.7. AM I LIKELY TO BUY A ROD MADE FROM INFERIOR CANE?

Not if it's been made in this country. Some imported rods are made from very poor cane, but all reputable British manufacturers buy the best sort. which comes from Tonkin in China.

The cane produced in Tonkin does vary a little in quality. Its rate of growth is extremely important. This in turn affects the thickness of the outer skin or 'wall'. Cane that grows very fast has too thin a skin and is too floppy for a fly-rod. Cane that grows very slowly, on the other hand, has too thick a skin and is too stiff. The rate of growth is fairly simple to judge. It shows in the spacing of the 'knots' (often called 'nodes') which appear as raised rings around any length of bamboo.

The ideal spacing between these nodes is *about* eighteen inches This varies a little because different rates of growth suit different rods. But if they are *much* farther apart, the cane has grown rather too quickly. And if they are much closer, too slowly.

A rod-manufacturer, when he receives the cane, can reject any pieces that he doesn't think are good enough. Some manufacturers are rather more particular about this than others, and a little variation in quality may occur here. But much of the raw cane used by different rod-makers does in fact come from the same sources (despite the many exotic names which it's given in fishing tackle catalogues).

Finished rods can indeed be good or fair or bad. But the difference nearly always lies far more in the processing and making-up of the cane, rather than in the raw material itself.

Some other Aspects of Rods

Q.8 WHY ARE SOME RODS MORE EXPENSIVE THAN OTHERS?

Let's dispose of one old wives' tale right away—the tale that

fishermen are made to pay a lot 'for the name'. It doesn't apply
to good rods. *All* rod-makers, both well-known and obscure, are
trying to produce rods at competitive prices these days. It's an
overcrowded trade and anyone who over-prices goes to the wall.

It is true that the price of a mass-produced rod does depend
to some extent on *quantity*. Very popular rods can often be
turned out in sufficient numbers to keep their price pretty low—
thanks to the economies of mass production. Conversely, a really
carefully-constructed or specialist rod, expensive to make and
sold only in small numbers, may appear rather high-priced by
comparison.

By far the most important elements in the cost of a rod,
however, are *the quality of the material from which it is made and the
amount of skilled time that is spent on it*. This applies to both cane
and glass rods, as follows:

(a) *Cane.* The raw cane processed by different manufacturers may not vary very much. But the *selection and
matching* certainly do. Every single piece of cane *should* be
carefully chosen to go with every other piece and to play
its proper part in a fine rod. This means a tremendous
amount of painstaking sorting—taking into account
every detail such as colour, knot-spacing and wall-
thickness. It takes time—and time is money.

The selection of the raw material is the first step. There
are many stages of production afterwards, during each
of which a rod can be made or marred. A good rod is
inspected at every stage—and rejected if it shows any
flaw.

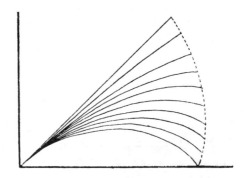

Diagram 2

After the rod has been nearly completed, one final question remains. Does it measure up exactly to the prototype? Another test is needed which is often carried out with a wall-chart like that shown in Diagram 2. Here a rod, finished except for fittings, can be set up against the wall-chart. The wall-chart shows the exact curves of the prototype in varying degrees of flexion. The new rod will only be put on sale if it can match these curves precisely.

(b) *Glass.* The construction of a good glass rod begins a long time before the glass actually arrives at the rod-maker's. First, the rod-maker has to choose a fibreglass manufacturer to work with. (Unless he has his own fibreglass factory, which is very rare.) There are a great many manufacturers to choose from, and the fibreglass they turn out varies considerably in quality. And in price too. (A rod-maker can always buy poor fibreglass at a knock-down price, but it won't produce a high-quality rod.)

So his choice of raw material is important. It may be supplied to him in the form of fibreglass 'cloth' from which he'll construct fibreglass tubes. See page 169. Or it may be supplied in the form of ready-made 'blanks'—lengths of tubular glass which have already been tapered. He will have laid down his precise requirements for length, diameter, taper, wall-thickness and so on. He'll reject any blanks that do not match his specifications. And the better he is, the more exacting will be his standards.

Then the glass blanks have to be 'finished'. This involves skilled labour. And when a good glass rod has been nearly completed, it will undergo the same sort of final test as a cane rod. It has to match its prototype in every detail.

(c) *Carbon-fibre.* The process of making a good carbon-fibre rod follows much the same sequence as for a glass rod, with two exceptions. One is that not *all* carbon-fibre rods start out as a 'cloth', though most do. The other exception is more important and has more bearing on the question of price. Carbon-fibre rods have thinner diameters than glass rods and have to be made to more demanding specifications, with smaller permissible tolerances. A higher degree of technical perfection is required, with more careful checking. This is one reason for the high cost of a good carbon-fibre rod. The other is the extra cost of the raw material. Carbon fibre is very expensive.

(d) *Quality/economy.* A fisherman *needn't* pay for top-quality material or the time of skilled labour.

It's easy enough for rod-makers to cut corners to make less expensive rods. They can be less careful in selecting good material. They can have fewer and less rigorous inspections. They can pass rods that vary from their prototypes. And they can make machines do nearly *all* the work—instead of just the work they're best fitted for. The result will always be a less perfect rod.

So what *is* the 'best bargain'? I think it must vary with the individual. If a man fishes frequently, and if his fishing requires him to cast well, he really can't afford *not* to have one of the best rods. It will certainly help his performance and hence his enjoyment. It will give him great pride of ownership. And he needn't consider himself extravagant in any way, because the rod will last him for a very long time. (He won't regret his choice and be tempted to buy a new rod. That's extravagance.)

But if a man simply wants an 'occasional' rod—something to throw into the back of his car when he goes on holiday—then he hardly needs one of the best rods. A reasonably-made rod will give him good service for many years. After all, he will not use it very often. And if his sport consists mainly of 'rough' fishing, the margin of extra casting capacity given by a first-rate rod is unnecessary. He can buy a less expensive rod, which still needn't be a 'cheap' and bad one, without depriving himself of any pleasure.

Q.9   HOW LONG A ROD DO I NEED?

Obviously different lengths of rod suit different sorts of fly-fishing. Here are some suggestions:

(a) *Still water.* Distance can be important to bank fishermen
     on all still waters except very small ones. This isn't to say
     that a stillwater fisherman won't catch plenty of fish quite
     close to him – even at his very feet – but his rod should have
     the *capacity* for distance, for those times when the fish are
     feeding quite far away.

     He'll therefore use a longish rod – usually between 9 feet
     and 10 feet – with power enough to handle a fairly heavy
     line. (A heavy line can gather more velocity than a light
     line for casting long distances.)

     He won't have a cane rod, because cane is too heavy for
     comfort in such a long rod. He'll use glass, or carbon fibre
     if he can afford it. Although the rod should be compara-
     tively powerful, it shouldn't be like a telegraph pole for
     two reasons. One is that a *very* stiff rod tends to tire the
     caster. And the other is that there'll be occasions when he
     wants to fish more delicately for fish rising close at hand, if
     possible with a lighter line. For this reason numbers of
     stillwater fishermen carry two rods. They may be the
     same length, but one will be powerful enough for a heavy
     line, while the other will be flexible enough for a lighter
     line.

(b) *Boat fishing.* A long rod helps you to dibble wet flies on
     the surface of the water when you're retrieving a cast.
     But the rod needn't be extra-powerful, because long
     distances aren't necessary when drifting. And the wind is
     always behind.

     A lightish rod of 9 feet to 10 feet 6 inches is ideal.

     (I must confess to a personal heresy here. I very much
     enjoy fishing a drift with a tiny 6 feet 6 inch rod. Playing
     loch trout on it is great sport. And casting all day is light
     work. But I can't pretend it's efficient—only an example
     of sheer idiosyncracy.)

(c) *Dry-fly rivers.* Distance is only occasionally important.
     Most experienced dry-fly fishermen would rather forget
     the odd out-of-range trout than burden themselves with
     unwieldy tackle. An unwieldy rod won't cast delicately.
     And the delicacy of dry-fly fishing is a great deal of its
     charm.

Partly for this reason, dry-fly rods have become significantly shorter over the past few decades. And the Americans, who've always used short light rods, may have influenced our thinking. But we seldom go as far as they do—down to under 6 feet.

Our grandfathers used rods of 10 feet or more. Halford recommended 10 feet 6 inches as a practical length, and even now there are some very long rods in use on the Test. But most good modern dry-fly rods are between 8 feet and 8 feet 9 inches. They are beautiful tools and a great improvement on their forerunners.

Then there are the little brooks, as opposed to rivers. The shortest feasible rod gives the most enjoyment on these—not to speak of a far better chance of casting successfully under overhanging branches. And of avoiding getting caught by bushes behind. Rods of 6 feet to 7 feet give wonderful opportunities for dexterity and pleasure.

All these dry-fly rods are also very good for fishing nymphs or upstream wet flies, when the same accuracy and delicacy are required.

(d) *Wet-fly rivers.* On broad wet-fly rivers a number of specialist wet-fly fishermen use a fairly long rod, up to 10 feet. This enables them to reach more holding-places for trout, and also to strike more quickly. The less line there is to lift off the water, the quicker the strike will be.

This may be the ideal, but for most of us a good dry-fly rod makes almost as good a wet-fly rod. Since accuracy and delicacy may not be so vital on a wet-fly stream, the rod needn't be of such high quality—but its length will be more or less the same. 8 feet 9 inches for average rivers. 6 feet—7 feet for brooks. 9 feet for wide rivers.

Q.10   IS IT BEST TO HAVE A TWO-PIECE OR THREE-PIECE ROD?

Theoretically, it's best to have a one-piece rod. Then there can be no interruption whatsoever in the smoothness of the action.

Some rods—up to 6 feet in length—are sold in a single piece.

They cast very nicely. But getting into a railway carriage with them is a tricky manoeuvre. And most fishermen, in any case, do need a longer rod. They have the following alternatives:

(a) *'Spliced' rods.* A 'spliced' rod is the nearest approach to a one-piece rod. It has two pieces but *no* ferrule—since the joints overlap and are taped together with special adhesive tape. Its casting action is very smooth but the taping does involve a good deal of trouble every time the rod is assembled or disassembled.

(b) *Two-piece rods.* Two-piece rods with one ferrule are the most popular nowadays. A single ferrule makes very little difference to the action. And two pieces take less time to put together than three.

(c) *Three-piece rods.* Modern ferrules don't in fact interrupt a rod's action so much as many people think. So fishermen who do a lot of travelling may choose three-piece rods for the sake of convenience. They can be very good indeed.

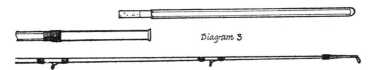

Diagram 3

(d) *'Staggered ferrule' rods.* The 'staggered ferrule' (above) is quite a recent development. A rod of this type has two pieces, the top-joint being a few inches longer than the butt-joint. In the rod-bag, the shortness of the butt-joint is compensated for by an extra-long stopper in the ferrule so that the rod-tip is protected. There is no interruption at all in the action of the *most important* part of a staggered ferrule rod—the top three-fifths. This is the part that flexes most and has the greatest effect on accuracy.

(e) *Spare tops.* Most rods are sold with one top, some with two. Even when a maker normally sells a rod with one top, he will usually provide another on request. A spare top is certainly an insurance against accident. But against this, experience shows that when the spare top is left alone in the rod-bag, that's where the accident often happens. Spare tops do not really lengthen the life of rods significantly. And they do make rods more expensive. They are not needed by many fishermen—except those who may be away from home for a long·time.

Fittings

Q.11. WHICH ARE THE BEST FERRULES?

Suction ferrules. These are almost universally used nowadays. At one time many good rods had more complicated ferrules which locked or screwed into position. But it was always admitted that they were heavier.

Today well-made suction ferrules—constructed from brass or 'German silver' —are so good that they will suit any trout flyrod. And they are light.

(Ferrules on the best rods are always turned and part-tapered by *hand*, and then fitted by hand. This is in fact one of the most skilled operations at a rod-factory.) There are two common designs for a suction ferrule:

(a) *Ordinary suction ferrule.* Sketch A below shows a typical suction ferrule for a cane rod. It is occasionally seen on glass rods too.

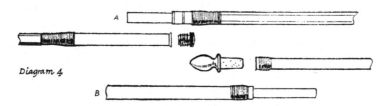

Diagram 4

(b) *Spigot ferrule.* Sketch B shows another type of suction ferrule which has become the normal type used for glass rods. It is the 'spigot' or 'glass-to-glass' ferrule. Here the ferrules are the other way round—with the male ferrule below the female ferrule. Both are made of fibreglass and are slightly tapered. The male ferrule is fitted by being pushed up the tube from below and then bonded firmly into place. The female ferrule is fitted into the butt of the upper joint.

(c) *Sleeve ferrule.* This was first used on carbon-fibre rods and is the lightest ferrule of all, also the least obvious to the eye. Imagine what the picture opposite the letter B (in Diagram 4) would look like if the male ferrule had no tyings and no interruption in the taper. It could then simply be pushed inside the tube at the rear end of the rod's top joint. This is a sleeve ferrule.

Again both parts of the ferrule are of similar material (such as carbon-to-carbon) so that the ferrule does not interrupt the action of the rod. The carbon fibre (or any other material) does need strengthening at both male and female ferrule to guard against breakage, but provided this is adequately done the ferrule is a first-rate one.

Some suction ferrules incorporate helpful extras. Here are two of them:

(a) A glass-to-glass (or carbon-to-carbon) ferrule has been developed which you assemble by inserting the male into the female ferrule, and then giving it a right angle turn. The turn creates a vacuum between the ferrules and holds them in position.

(b) Some makes of ferrule have a pair of coloured 'indicator spots'—one on the male and one on the female ferrule. When the spots are opposite each other, the rod-rings are aligned. It's a useful addition.

Q.12. WHICH TYPE OF ROD-HANDLE IS THE BEST?

A comfortable one. If a handle feels at all uncomfortable when you first pick up a rod, it will feel doubly or triply so at the end of a day's fishing. Although the exact shapes may vary a good deal, the main types are shown on page 160.

(a) *Tapered.* Sketches A and B in Diagram 5 both show tapered handles. Sometimes they're called double-tapered handles, or cigar-shaped handles. It's best to avoid handles that taper too *steeply* in front. If you cast with your thumb on top, the thumb needs something to push against. (If you cast with your forefinger on top, it doesn't matter.)

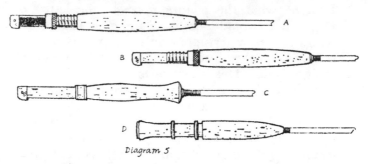

Diagram 5

(b) *'Shaped'*. Sketch C shows a 'shaped' or 'anatomical' handle. The fatter part fits the palm of the hand. The thumb lies in the thinner part and is held there by the swelling at the end. It is ideal for casting with the thumb on top. Provided the handle in question is sensibly shaped and does fit the hand, it is quite excellent.

(c) *Midge*. The handle shown in Sketch D is usually confined to short 'midge' rods. (The term 'midge' should only be applied to rods weighing 2 oz. or less.) In order to have as much cane as possible for casting, the handle has to be kept short too. This is a matter of necessity for midge rods—which mustn't weigh more than 2 oz.—but it's rather uncomfortable and should be avoided on longer rods.

Q.13. WHICH IS THE MOST SUITABLE REEL-FITTING?

There's a choice between four main types of reel-fitting. Apart from good looks, the important considerations are lightness and security (making sure that the reel doesn't fall off at a critical moment). The four types are shown in Diagram 5.

(a) *Screw-grip*. This is sometimes called a 'built-in screw-grip' and is shown in Sketch A. A locking ring screws down against the reel from above, securing it in a stationary slot. Or it may screw up against the reel from below.

Sometimes you find not just one locking ring but two. This type is undoubtedly the safest reel-fitting.

It is also the heaviest fitting. But the weight is really only a disadvantage with very light rods. With a heavier rod it makes little enough difference. After all, the reel itself will probably weigh 4–6 oz.

And there's one other aspect. The most tiring thing about any rod is its top-heaviness. It is this top-heaviness —rather than the overall weight of the rod—that tires the arm and wrist. Extra weight at the *middle or tip* of a rod is bad, because it only increases top-heaviness. But a little extra weight at the butt is less important. (It even helps to make a very long rod balance better in the hand.)

(b) *Skeleton screw-grip.* This is shown in Sketch B. The reel lies on the cork of the handle, and is screwed by a locking ring against a slot in the butt-cap. (With either screw-grip, it is wrong for the thread of the screw to be too fine and narrow. If it is, the locking ring may jam.) Type B is virtually as safe as Type A, and it is a little lighter.

(c) *Sliding ring.* Here (see Sketch C) there is no screw at all. A sliding ring wedges the reel into the stationary slot and holds it there. The reel lies on the cork itself. This fitting is reasonably secure, and it is lighter than either of the screw-grips. It is ideal whenever lightness is important.

(d) *Midge.* Two sliding rings on cork. See Sketch D. This is the lightest of all reel-fittings, but it secures the reel least firmly. It is usually seen on 'midge' rods, when every fraction of an ounce is a vital matter. It is not to be recommended for other rods.

Whenever casting is continuous and energetic—as in reservoir fishing—the question of security should have high priority. Reservoir rods are best made with the safest fitting—that is, one of the screw-grips. These are also best for boat fishermen on lochs. For other forms of flyfishing any of the reel-fittings *except* D will prove perfectly efficient.

Finally, a word about the materials used for reel-fittings. The 'reel-seating'—which is the correct name for the place on the handle where the reel lies—may be of aluminium or plastic. (If

it doesn't consist of the cork itself.) Both are good materials,
plastic being the lighter. All locking and sliding rings should be
of aluminium. It is an advantage for the aluminium to be
'anodised'. This treatment protects the outer surface against
corrosion.

Q.14. ARE SOME ROD-RINGS BETTER THAN OTHERS?

Different rings are best for different parts of the rod.

(a) *Tip-rings.* Here are the two most usual type of tip-ring:
Type A is excellent. It's made from hardened stainless
steel or chrome and is sometimes called an American-

Diagram 6

type ring. Its great advantage is that it's always wide
enough to let any line through without friction—even one
of the modern large-diameter floating lines. (This is
important, because friction reduces distance and causes
wear.) It also lets the line-to-leader knot pass through
easily. Rings that do not are a nuisance. You so often
have to rest the rod-butt on the ground while you reach
up to free the knot from the tip. And they can have more
dangerous consequences if you happen to reel the knot
through the tip-ring while you're playing a fish.

Type B, in its smaller versions, does have this fault. If
it's large enough, however, it is perfectly suitable in
shape—though the materials from which it's made vary a
little in durability. This ring is normally referred to by the
name of one of these materials—'Agate' or 'Agatine' or
'Agatipe' or 'Aqualite' or 'Sintox'. All of them, like
hardened steel, are anti-friction materials—tough but
smooth.

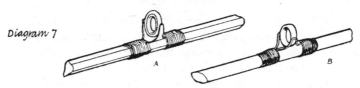

Diagram 7

(b) *Butt-rings*. Above are the two types of ring most often used as butt-rings. Type A is similar to tip-ring B, and is made of the same materials. Type B is made of hardened stainless steel. The most important aspect of a butt-ring is again the avoidance of friction, especially when line is stripped sideways through it during casting. Both types fulfil this requirement.

Diagram 8

(c) *Intermediates*. Types A and B above are 'intermediate' rings. These can be 'snake rings' as in A or 'full-open bridge rings' as in B. They do not have to withstand so much pull as tip-rings or butt-rings. Their object is to let the line go through as freely as possible and both succeed in this. Snake rings are the lighter of the two types and are better for light rods.

(d) *Keeper rings*. Some rods also have a small 'keeper ring' near the handle. The fly can be lodged in it when the rod and tackle are assembled. Many people, however, find it just as easy to keep the fly in one of the ordinary rod-rings. (The cork handle shouldn't be used for this purpose.)

Q.15. DO 'TYINGS' HELP TO HOLD A CANE ROD TOGETHER?

They shouldn't *have* to. Once upon a time they fulfilled this purpose, but rod-making glues and resins have improved beyond recognition since then. Any rod-maker worth his salt will use a good glue and construct his rod in such a way that the cane sections will *never* come apart. Today, tyings are for decoration.

In the old days silk tyings were also used to hide faulty joins or flaws in the cane. And this leads to a point worth making. Good cane rods are better today than they have ever been. You will hear many people running them down. They talk about shortages of material and craftsmen. These shortages do exist— but they are not nearly so significant as the fact that many processes have been vastly improved by up-to-date techniques. And the design of rods has become better and better over the years.

Good Rods and Bad

Q.16. WHAT IS SO 'SKILFUL' ABOUT BUILDING A CANE ROD?

There are a number of stages in the making of a built-cane rod. They are all important and all need a good deal of skill. Here is a brief outline (which doesn't really do the craftsman justice) of the various stages:

(a) The raw canes are received and examined. They are thicker than most people imagine—3 inches or more in diameter. Any canes which are considered unsatisfactory are rejected.

(b) The cane is split in half (lengthways). This allows the sap to evaporate while it 'matures'.

(c) The cane is 'baked' in ovens (usually gas or electric) in order to harden it. It emerges stiffer and tougher. This process is also called 'tempering' or 'curing'.

(d) Individual half-canes are selected for the joints (i.e. butt, middle, top) of particular rods. Two per joint are needed but they cannot be two halves of one length. The half-canes must be deliberately 'mis-matched' so that the knots are staggered. (See Diagram 10 opposite.) But they should be exactly alike in quality, diameter, colour and stiffness. Stiffness is governed by the thickness of the outer skin or 'wall'. Thick-walled cane is stiffer than thin-walled cane, and each can be useful for different types of rod—or for different parts of the same rod. The wall or skin is the strongest part of the cane.

(e) The half-canes are split again (lengthways). This process can be carried out either by hand (for a 'straight grain' rod) or by precision machines. Then three sections (see A below) are selected from each of the half-canes. It is these six sections which will later be triangulated and fitted together to make a finished joint. At B we see them end-on.

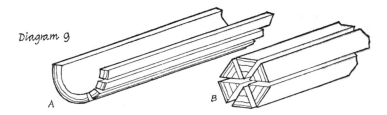

Diagram 9

(You might expect that the angle of cut would be 360° divided by six—that is, 60°. In fact, sections are deliberately cut to about $61\frac{1}{2}°$, leaving a carefully calculated space in the centre when they are fitted together. This space is filled with special glue to strengthen the rod. The $61\frac{1}{2}°$ angle is sometimes pointed out as an example of slipshod craftsmanship. In fact, it is a deliberate process which *improves* a rod's performance.)

(f) The six cane sections are now tapered by hand or by machine. Other terms used are 'milling' or 'planing'. As little as possible of the outside skin should be cut away. The outside skin is what gives a cane rod its strength and it must be carefully preserved. The exact taper will have been laid down in the design for the rod.

(g) The sections are then fitted and glued together. (The glueing process is sometimes called 'cementing'.) The knots along each section should appear about half-way between the knots of the next.

Diagram 10

Sketch A in Diagram 10 shows the correct spacing. Sketch B shows how a rod would appear if the knots coincided. Each cluster of knots would interrupt the action badly and make a weak point in the rod.

(h) The sections are bound or wrapped while the glue 'sets'. The rod-maker now has his 'blanks' of built cane and will keep them in this form till he needs them.

(i) The blanks are cleaned. Wrappings and excess glue are scraped off.

(j) The blanks are carefully and meticulously checked. Precise adjustments in length are made. (This affects the overall diameter too. The diameter increases or decreases according to whether length-adjustments are made at the tip or the butt.)

(k) Ferrules are fitted.

(l) The flexion of the rod is tested against that of the prototype, often by hanging weights on the tip and comparing the curves. (See Diagram 2.) If a rod is to be a high-quality one, it has to compare exactly. An 'average' rod is allowed a little more latitude. Some of the poorer rods are never tested at all.

(m) Cork handles and reel fittings are added. Sometimes the handles are ready-made. But the handles of all the best rods are constructed from a number of individual cork rings which the craftsman shapes by hand, and then fits over the butt of each rod. (See diagram below). This is the only completely satisfactory way of ensuring that the cane will never shift inside the handle.

Diagram 11

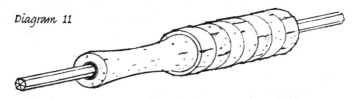

(n) The final processes consist of weatherproof-varnishing and the fitting of rod-rings. The varnish is sometimes dulled to prevent any glitter which might frighten fish—

though this is a very hypothetical advantage. The varnish should be flexible so as not to crack. The rod is now complete.

Q.17. WHAT IS 'IMPREGNATION'?

One British manufacturer is a leading exponent of this process. The details of it are 'trade secrets' but in essence it involves soaking rod-blanks in baths of special resin. Each blank has a given number of immersions, at given temperatures, for given periods of time. The resin then fills all the tiny pores and cavities in and between the fibres of the cane. In fact it 'impregnates' the material.

As a result, the cane becomes to all intents and purposes completely solid. It is therefore stronger and more powerful, and less likely to take on a distortion or 'set'. Although it is a little heavier, its extra strength allows it to be used in far smaller diameters and the result is a rod which is light for its power. Impregnated rods need no varnish and are as waterproof as glass or carbon-fibre rods.

Q.18. ARE HAND-MADE CANE RODS ALWAYS THE BEST?

No. There are very good and very bad hand-made rods. It naturally depends on the individual craftsman, as well as on his choice of materials.

Again, we sometimes speak of 'hand-made' rods as if all other rods were produced *entirely* by machines. This isn't so. Many of the best rods are partly made by hand and partly by machine. The machines are used not only for economy, but also because they carry out certain processes exceptionally well. The various processes in rod-building can be broken down as follows:

(a) *Hand Processes.* Some processes do indeed need great human skill and judgement and are best carried out by hand. These include the selection of the raw material, the exact matching of every section and joint to suit their companions in a rod, the addition of ferrules and handles, and a close inspection at every stage.

All hand-made rods, of course, get this attention as a matter of routine. *But so do all good 'machine-made' rods.*

(b) *Splitting the cane.* The main difference between the two methods of rod-building lies in the process of splitting the raw cane (into the six long sections that make *built* cane) and then in planing the sections to precisely the right taper. This can be done either by a hand-craftsman or a machine.

The hand-craftsman can and does claim that he makes a stronger rod—a 'straight-grain' rod. When he splits the bamboo, he can see that the split follows its most natural course, straight along the grain of the cane. You can do much the same with a penknife and a piece of ordinary bamboo.

A machine, now, may cut very slightly *across* the grain. At first sight, this seems to give the hand-craftsman a definite advantage—but his straight-grain sections often pose him a problem at a later stage. They are liable to have slightly wavy edges (as will ordinary bamboo split with a penknife) and he may not be able to find other sections which fit exactly when they are laid alongside. As a result, he often has to plane *away* his straight-grain edges.

Machines are very accurate. They will cut and plane bamboo to a tolerance of about a one-thousandth of an inch. And the sections—although they aren't straight-grain sections—always fit very closely together.

It's six of one and half-a-dozen of the other.

(c) *Finishing.* Certain hand processes can also improve the final appearance of a rod. Hand-varnishing, for instance, can make sure it's all the same colour. (Though one expert I know always suspects this is a cover-up for badly-matched raw material!) And the knots can be hand-pressed to make them less visible. Neither process affects the actual performance of a rod.

There is no doubt that a hand-craftsman—*if* he has the skill and is given the time—can turn out a wonderful rod. But good 'machine-made' rods are in no way inferior. Much of their building will have been carried out by hand.

Q.19. WHAT IS IMPORTANT IN BUILDING A TUBULAR ROD?

By far the most important component is—the material. Carbon fibre and fibreglass are made in a bewildering variety of forms. And they differ immensely in quality.

A rod-maker has to determine the exact sort of material he wants for a rod. He then has to find a manufacturer who can make it well enough, at a price he considers right. Here is a cut-down account of how the tubes are made:

(a) The basic material is a 'cloth' of carbon or glass fibres. The fibres can be of many shapes and sizes, and they can be arranged in many ways to make up the cloth. And the cloth can be either thick or thin. (Some carbon-fibre rods don't start off as a 'cloth', but these are in the minority.)

(b) The tube is made by wrapping the cloth round a 'mandrel'. This is a tapered object not unlike a fishing rod in shape, but made of rolled steel. Its dimensions dictate the diameter and taper of the tube. It therefore has to be very carefully designed.

(c) Before the cloth is put on the mandrel, it has to be cut so that *exactly* the right amount of material is eventually wrapped round.

(d) The wall-thickness of the tube is determined by the thickness of the cloth and by the number of times it is wrapped round the mandrel. A thin-walled tube is lighter than a thick-walled tube. But it is usually less strong, though strength does vary with the construction of the material itself. Rod-makers are continually search-ing for ways to combine minimum weight with maximum strength and power.

(e) Once the cloth is on the mandrel, it is treated with resin. Various resins with various properties are available. Or a mixture of several resins can be used. Both the amount and the type of resin have to be carefully worked out.

(f) The cloth, still on the mandrel and now treated with resin, is 'baked' in an oven. This hardens it into the sort of tubular carbon fibre or glass used for rod-making.

(g) The mandrel is removed, leaving a tubular 'blank'. It is delivered in this form to the rod-finisher. Whereas a cane blank is made for each *joint* in a rod, a tubular blank is usually made for a whole rod. Most carbon-fibre or glass rods only need a single blank.

The rod-finisher will carefully check the blanks when they arrive—to see that they match the specifications he has laid down. The better the finished rod is to be, the more scrupulous will be the checking. Unsatisfactory blanks will be rejected.

Standards for carbon-fibre rods are a good deal more rigorous than those for glass rods. The fine diameter of a carbon-fibre rod, for one thing, means that very little tolerance can be allowed. Throughout the whole construction of a carbon-fibre rod the utmost technical skill has to be exercised, combined with ultra-careful checking at various stages. Although the method of making a carbon-fibre blank may be similar to making a glass blank, the whole process has to be more exacting.

(One point worth noting is that the butts of glass blanks—and hence of glass rods—are frequently fatter than those of other rods. For technical reasons, the diameter of the tube usually has to be fairly wide at the butt. It is not necessarily a sign of a bad rod.)

The trimming of the blanks and the addition of fittings will follow the same course as for cane rods. So will the comparison of a good finished rod with a prototype.

Q.20.   CAN I HAVE A ROD SPECIALLY MADE
        FOR ME?

Yes. It's perfectly feasible to order and get a 'made-to-measure' rod in cane. It's more difficult to acquire one in carbon fibre or glass, because its design may be limited by the glass 'blanks' available to the manufacturer. But even so, it's possible.

The trouble is that it's seldom worth-while. If you're prepared to experiement over a long period of time, it can be an intriguing experience, but the 'invention' of a rod is never so simple as it sounds. The first few samples are liable to be expensive mistakes. Here are two of the reasons:

(a) *A matter of time.* It's worth remembering that master-designers may take several years to develop a good rod. Many prototypes will be tried out and rejected before the taper and action are entirely satisfactory.

(b) *Tapers.* Even a simple taper has to be calculated carefully. And tapers aren't always simple—they can become prodigiously complicated. Most rods are 'continuous taper' rods, which taper evenly and regularly from butt to tip. But other rods have a 'compound taper'.

The difference—in an exaggerated form—can be illustrated like this:

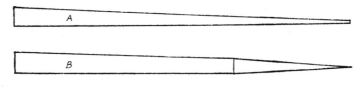

Diagram 12

Sketch A demonstrates a continuous taper, and Sketch B a compound taper. The effect of this sort of compound taper is to stiffen the butt and give the whole rod more tip action. Other sorts of compound taper have other effects on the action. Compound tapers can be very effectively used in some trout rods.

Q.21. CAN ONE TELL ANYTHING BY WAGGLING A ROD IN A SHOP?

Not much. Not really enough. Most people waggle rods in showrooms and it's rather dangerous to ask them why they're doing it—because it's ten to one they won't be able to answer. The only entirely satisfactory way to try out a rod is by casting with it.

Rod-Actions

Q.22.   WHAT ARE ALL THESE 'ACTIONS'— 'TIP ACTION' AND SO ON?

There are a great many so-called 'actions'. The phrases that describe them aren't always very meaningful. Some must have been made up just for advertising purposes.

But 'tip action' is a standard term and a good descriptive phrase. And so are its brethren phrases 'butt action' and 'middle action'. They describe the different ways in which a rod can flex and bend. Given an equal tension, three different rods might bend like this:

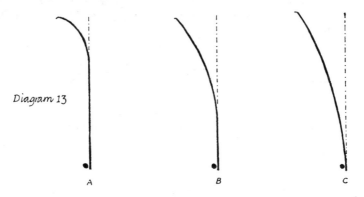

Diagram 13

A   B   C

Sketch A illlustrates a tip-action rod. B is a middle-action rod. And C is a butt-action rod.

Q.23.   WHICH IS THE BEST ACTION?

There isn't any. Rods with different actions are designed for different purposes and for different types of flyfishing. So the action that's best for one man and his fishing mightn't suit the next man nearly so well.

For instance, you seldom see a *pronounced* tip-action rod—or a pronounced butt-action rod—because each of them serves only a very limited purpose. Most people quite rightly choose more versatile rods. These will in fact be 'middle-to-tip-action' rods, or middle-action rods, or 'middle-to-butt-action' rods.

Q.24. WHAT DO THESE DIFFERENT ACTIONS *DO?*

The actual functions of the various actions can't be explained in a nutshell—or not if they're to be understood properly. The explanation involves discussing a few casting dynamics.

The following will talk mainly about tip-action and butt-action rods—without referring often to middle-action rods—in order to make the explanation clearer. (But it's worth remembering that nearly all good rods do avoid the two extremes.)

To start with the obvious, every flyrod bends. It bends most easily at the tip, and progressively less easily as the curve goes down towards the butt. (Hence the term 'progressive action'—which has sometimes been used to describe a particular rod. In fact, it applies to all the tapered rods ever made!) But rods can be tapered in different ways, with various results.

(a) *Alternative tapers.* If you give a rod-maker a certain length and weight specification, he can still vary the taper by altering the relative thickness of the butt to the tip. To exaggerate considerably for the sake of demonstration, there could be two very different tapers like this:

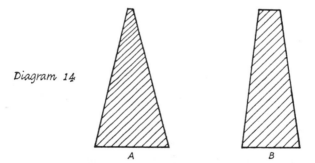

Diagram 14

A   B

In fact, if you cut out two pieces of paper in these shapes and bend them, they will caricature 'tip-action' and 'butt-action' rods. Taper A bends easily enough at the narrow end of the paper (remember a rod never quite tapers to a pin-point) but it takes a good deal more force to bend the middle and butt. The most U-shaped part of the curve tends to be high up.

Taper B will be quite different. The middle and butt

of the paper will begin to bend without nearly so much pressure. And the most U-shaped part of the curve will be farther down towards the butt.

(b) *Alternative actions.* A rod made on the principle of taper A—that is, tapering from a broad butt to a thin and narrow tip—will of course be a tip-action rod. And a rod that tapers gradually as in B—with the minimum difference between butt and tip—will be a butt-action rod. Yet the overall amount and weight of material used remains exactly the same.

(c) *Alternative casting curves.* The casting actions of the rods will be quite different. The curves made by tip- and butt-action rods (used with exactly the same force and leverage) will look like these:

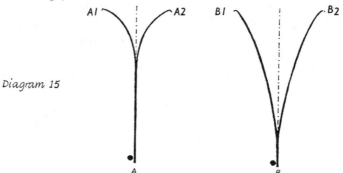

Diagram 15

(d) *Alternative arcs and loops.* The distance travelled by the tip of a rod (e.g. A1 to A2) is called the 'arc'. If the rod-tip travels only a short distance, it's a 'narrow arc'. A longer distance—and it's a 'wide arc'.

As any casting instructor will confirm, the width or narrowness of the arc dictates how the line curves as it goes through the air. The part where the curve is sharpest is the 'loop'. A narrow arc casts a 'narrow loop' or 'tight loop' and a wide arc casts a 'wide loop' like this:

Diagram 16

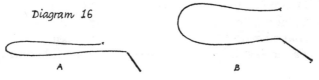

The narrower the loop, the better for distance. A narrow loop offers less air and wind resistance, and so helps the line to go faster and farther. A wide loop won't cut through the air nearly so well. And it will be affected much more by the wind.

Now look at Diagram 15 again. The distance between A1 and A2 is shorter than that between B1 and B2. So rod A has the narrower arc. Tip-action rods do describe narrower arcs and so cast narrower loops than butt-action rods—given that the leverage is identical. (But with a different leverage, a butt-action rod *can* cast an equally narrow loop. A casting instructor could explain how.)

In conclusion, it is extremely difficult to avoid thinking about tip action and butt action in rather exaggerated terms. But it can be very misleading. An excessively 'tippy' rod would have a thick pole for a butt and a slender, fragile tip. It would cast badly and it might break near its reed-like tip. Equally, an excessively 'butty' rod would be far too floppy. The only truthful 'action' one could claim for it would be a 'spaghetti action'.

Q.25. HOW WILL THESE ACTIONS AFFECT *MY* CASTING?

Although a tip-action rod and a butt-action rod can transmit the same total power to a line, they do it in different ways. You'll find that several aspects of casting are affected, as follows:

a) *Speed*. A butt-action rod is a 'slow' rod. A tip-action rod is a 'fast' rod. This is because a tip action *concentrates* energy.

Sketch A on page 176 shows a tip-action rod—and Sketch B a butt-action rod. Each sketch shows one of the rods flexing as it makes a backward cast. The shaded areas represent the two ways in which energy is transmitted to the line. It's assumed that the same force is activating each rod.

The difference can be seen. The shaded area in A

(tip action) is considerably smaller than in B (butt-action) and the energy is more *concentrated*. It is delivered in a shorter period of time. Tip action provides *quicker* acceleration.

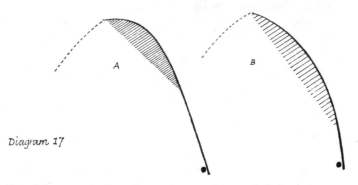

Diagram 17

(b) *Distance.* A fast tip-action rod is a definite asset to any good caster who needs distance.

Distance depends above all else on the *momentum* of the line when it is 'shot' through the air. And this in turn depends on two separate factors: first, the weight of the line—and second, the speed at which it is travelling. If two lines with a different weight are travelling at the same speed, the heavier one will 'shoot' farther. And if two identical lines are travelling at different speeds—the one to travel farther will be the one travelling faster.

The ideal, then, is to have the heaviest practicable line travelling at the fastest possible speed.

Butt-action rods are of course slow—and they're unsuitable for handling heavy lines. Fast tip-action rods, on the other hand, work best with heavy lines. (The reasons why are given in (Q.26.) So tip-action rods can achieve greater distances.

Q.26. THEN WHY BOTHER ABOUT BUTT-ACTION RODS?

For several reasons. Rods with a bit of butt action have plenty to offer. After all, it isn't everyone who regards long-distance

casting as the only sort of pleasure to be had out of fishing.
It's rather tiring.

(a) *Ease of casting*. Although a tip-action rod will help a
fisherman to cast farther, it does demand more effort.
This is because the *whole* rod won't work—all the way
down to the butt—unless it is flexed pretty powerfully.
As Diagram 14 demonstrated, the butt of a tip-action
rod is always relatively thick, so more energy is needed
to bend it.

As opposed to this, the bottom part of a butt-action
or middle-action rod flexes quite easily. A fisherman
can make *every* part of these rods work for him—even
if they're quite long rods—without wearing himself out.

(b) *Delicacy*. A tip-action rod always needs a relatively
heavy line. Only a heavy line will gain enough velocity
to flex the rod properly. But heavy lines sometimes
come down rather heavily on the water. Butt-action
rods will flex with lighter lines. (In fact they're too
slow to keep heavy lines moving through the air.) So
butt-action and middle-action rods are ideal for short-
to medium-length casts—and for greater delicacy.

(c) *Accuracy*. A rod with some butt action wins here, so long
as there is no *strong* wind to blow the line off-course. This
is because middle- or butt-action rods 'dampen' the
force of a cast *slowly*. This gradual dampening helps a
fisherman to make his fly hover over a precise spot and
touch down on it lightly.

(d) *Casting into the wind*. How about casting into a wind? It's
been shown already how casting into a wind requires a
'narrow loop'. Both tip- and butt-action rods are
capable of casting narrow loops—if used correctly. A
tip-action rod helps by providing line-velocity as well,
but a good butt-action rod will cope with *most* winds.

Q.27. CAN YOU SUM UP THE ADVANTAGES OF TIP-ACTION AND BUTT-ACTION RODS?

Pronounced tip-action rods are best left to long-distance casters.
They're *extra*-fast. A professional can build up a very high line-

velocity with them, and so get distance. He may expend a great deal of energy every time he makes a cast—but a professional seldom has to cast all day. And his casting muscles will be well developed.

The usefulness of *pronounced* butt-action rods is equally limited. They can cast a relatively light line with considerable accuracy. But they will never cast it any distance—unless they're very long and heavy. Long butt-action rods are sometimes used by powerful men on reservoirs—but they are hard work.

For practical fishing, rods that *incline* towards tip action or butt action are infinitely better. They can be described as middle-to-tip-action rods or middle-to-butt-action rods, and they differ as follows:

(a) *A middle-to-tip-action rod* can be excellent whenever long casting takes first priority. It is particularly good for throwing a long, heavy line into a strong wind. But take care that the rod is not too long or heavy or stiff for you to flex properly.

(b) *A middle-to-butt-action rod* is ideal for many purposes. It is slow enough to be both accurate and delicate, and it will cast a fair way even into a wind. It will make all-day casting an effortless business. It needn't have an over-weight line. And its deliberate, unjerky action is extremely smooth and pleasant.

Now just a word about materials. Apart from carbon fibre, they are *not* equally suitable for the different actions.

(a) *Carbon fibre*, as I've hinted above, is the most versatile of materials. It can be made into middle-to-butt action rods, middle action rods or middle-to-tip action rods. They will have slender butts, not fat ones. And carbon fibre can also handle a wide range of line-weights.

(b) *Glass* is a very suitable material for rods that incline towards tip action. Glass rods are not only lighter than cane rods, but also a little stronger and stiffer at the butt. So a glass rod can handle a slightly heavier line, which will in fact help to bring the butt into play. And it's been shown earlier that a tip-action rod *needs* a heavy line. What is more, a heavy line actually *improves* the action of a glass rod—because it helps to deaden the natural bounce of the material.

(c) *Cane* is a perfect material for middle-to-butt-action rods. Even though cane is a trifle heavier than glass, the relative 'easiness' of a butt action makes casting light work. And because it needn't have a thick butt, it is simple to make a cane rod with a butt action. As a material, cane is excellent for accuracy. So is a butt action—and it provides delicacy too. The material and the action suit each other perfectly.

The above explains why many of the best *glass* rods have a middle-to-tip action, and why many of the best *cane* rods have a middle-to-butt action.

Q.28. HOW ABOUT 'DRY-FLY ACTION' AND 'WET-FLY ACTION'?

The term 'dry-fly action' refers to middle-to-butt-action rods. These rods provide the delicacy and accuracy that dry-fly fishing needs more than any other sort of flyfishing.

The term 'wet-fly action' is a very loosely-used one. In catalogues it is sometimes applied to rather floppy rods. It is likely that one or two manufacturers refer to their first-grade rods as 'dry-fly action' rods, and to their second-grade rods as 'wet-fly action' rods. But the fact is that good dry-fly rods and good wet-fly rods needn't be very different as regards action.

Q.29. WHERE DO 'POWERFUL ACTION' AND 'SUPPLE ACTION' AND 'AMERICAN ACTION' COME IN?

We fishermen need a ten-ton dictionary of rod-terms!

(a) *Powerful action.* The phrase 'powerful action' really means that the whole rod is powerful. The *power* of a rod depends on the quality and weight of the material that goes into it—*not* on whether it's a tip-action or a butt-action rod. The best-quality material will be the most powerful for its weight. And with any given material, the heavier and stiffer a rod is—the more potential power it will have. 'Potential' is the operative word—since very stiff and heavy rods cannot be flexed by ordinary fishermen.

(b) *Supple action.* A 'supple action' implies that a rod inclines not to be very stiff. The adjectives 'limber' and 'easy' are frequently used as alternatives.

(c) *American action.* The term 'American action' describes rods with some tip action. For a long time Americans have been accustomed to rather shorter and tippier rods than our own. An 'American-type' or 'American-style' rod will incline towards tip action.

Q.30. CAN I DO WITH ONLY ONE FLYROD?

Naturally you need only one rod if your fishing is confined to a single type. If you want a 'general purpose' rod it can't be *the* best for every sort of fly-fishing. But it can certainly be adequate for many sorts.

A rod of about 9 feet, capable of casting a No. 6 or No. 7 line, is generally considered to be the best type of all-rounder. It's not too long or cumbersome for rivers, yet it's 'man enough' to cope with a lot of stillwater flyfishing—even though it may not be absolutely *the* ideal for either. It would be a bit awkward, however, on little brooks and streams.

On the whole, if you do two different sorts of fishing it's wise to have two inexpensive rods—each one being the right tool for its job—rather than a single expensive rod. This is another area where glass can be very useful. You can acquire two glass rods for the price of one carbon-fibre rod, and be sure that you're not being unduly handicapped by your equipment.

Q.31. HOW CAN ONE TELL WHETHER A ROD IS WELL-MADE OR NOT?

It is easier to judge a cane rod than a tubular rod. Whereas the comparative quality of tubular carbon-fibre or glass lies largely in the unseen make-up of the fibres, the quality of a cane rod is often revealed by the building of it. Here are some tell-tale signs:

(a) A built-cane rod is hexagonal. It has six 'facets'. These facets—when you examine them—should be exactly equal in width.

(b) The rod should be clearly hexagonal all along. If it appears more *circular* than hexagonal near the tip, too much of the valuable outer skin may have been cut away during the planing process.

(c) There will be traces of the original knots at intervals along each section. If more than three of these (out of a maximum of six) occur at the same point on the rod, the cane has been badly matched. See Diagram 10.

(d) The cane should not distort easily. This can be tested by *bending* the rod-tip for a moment and then 'sighting' along the rod. You'll have given the tip a slight curve or 'set'. But if the rod is then flicked two or three times, this will straighten out of its own accord. If it does not straighten out, the cane is weak and will distort easily.

(After a cane rod has been used for some time, it often does develop a 'set' at the tip. This is quite normal and nothing to worry about. It is caused by the owner's casting action. A rod which is used by a right-hander tends to develop a slight set to the right. One used by a left-hander may have a set to the left.)

(e) The rod-tip should not vibrate too much. If it is given a quick firm flick it should come to rest fairly soon. It won't do so immediately—but neither should it quiver back and forth for any length of time. If it does, it will cast very inaccurately.

So far as tubular rods are concerned, only the last of these little tests has any significance. But it is worth carrying out—because the tip of an inferior glass rod will vibrate badly. Also bear in mind that the majority of good *glass* rods incline towards a relatively stiff action, which allows them to carry the heavy lines that suit them so well.

Fibreglass is a variable material. Even an expert will hesitate to pick up a glass rod and pronounce judgement on it instantly. It's much more difficult for an ordinary layman. But two common failings of bad glass rods are a bit too much vibration

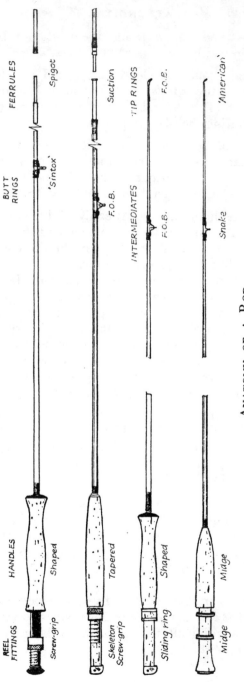

ANATOMY OF A ROD

all along and a general sogginess. These are not hard to detect and avoid.

When you first pick up a carbon-fibre rod, it'll almost certainly *feel* rather stiff. But that's only because the material's so light that there isn't enough weight in the tip to allow it to 'swing' of its own accord. It's a very different story when you arm the rod with a line and start casting. It'll then flex as it should, but not before. Carbon-fibre rods are the most difficult of all to judge from a waggle in a shop.

If a good manufacturer has staked his reputation on a tubular rod, it's always reassuring. Several good makers are devoting their time and skill to tubular carbon-fibre and glass these days, and their products are usually first-rate.

Section 2

Reels

Flyreels are as intricately designed as rods—but their finer points are of far less interest to a flyfisherman. It's well worth knowing a bit about rods—for the sake of choosing them well, for the sake of taking pride in them, and for the sake of casting a little better. But no one need lose any sleep over being unable to run a reel factory.

A reel plays its most important role when it's being used for reservoir fishing. There its capability can be critical. Large trout can run great distances in the open water of reservoirs, and it's then that reels are put to the test. The bigger the trout, the harder the test—and the greater the disappointment if a reel fails.

The mechanics of reels don't constitute vital information. Even so, a few technical terms will be explained in this section. That's because a good many catalogues—with their stress on spindles, pawls, ratchets and ball-races—could probably do with a little translation.

The Purpose of Reels

Q.32. IS IT THE MAIN JOB OF A REEL TO 'BALANCE' THE ROD?

No. 'Balancing the rod' used to be considered the be-all and end-all of a reel. This theory has been disproved for some time. *The most important function of a reel is to hold the right size of line plus its backing.*

'Balancing' is secondary. But it shouldn't be written off. A long and heavy rod, in particular, needs a relatively heavy reel. This will *counter*-balance the top-heaviness of the rod in the hand, and it will be less tiring to use.

Most medium-weight and all light rods aren't top-heavy enough to be tiring. Then the lightest practicable reel is the best reel. Extra weight in the hand only makes casting more wearisome. A reservoir reel may weigh 7 or 8 oz. But a light-weight reel can weigh as little as 3 oz., and an average reel weighs 4½–6 oz.

The reel must be sturdy. It must hold enough line and backing for your type of fishing. But within these limitations, let it be light.

Q.33. WHAT SHOULD I LOOK FOR IN CHOOSING A REEL?

There's a saying on the other side of the Atlantic 'Match the reel to the fish'. That's not bad advice. The most important thing to look for in any reel is its line-capacity. It must be able to carry enough line and backing for the trout you expect— or hope—to catch. But it shouldn't be needlessly large, or it will be needlessly heavy.

If you're fishing a reservoir with trophy trout in it you will need a reel with enough capacity for about 100 yards of backing You may not see the backing very often. But you'll be glad of it when the trout of a lifetime starts making for the far shore.

On small rivers even a large trout can't run very far. Often you can follow him if he does. A heavy reel would only be a burden, especially on a light rod. You can do with a smaller reel and less backing.

The capacity of a reel depends not only on the diameter of

the spool, but also on the width of the drum (see Anatomy of a
Reel on page 192).. A small reel, suitable for brook fishing,
might have a 3¼ inch spool. But a reel for a reservoir, or for a
sea trout river with the chance of a salmon, could have a
3¾ inch spool. A medium-sized reel, for ordinary dry-fly or
wet-fly rivers, might have a spool of 3½ inches. Drums are
usually divided into 'narrow', 'standard' and 'wide'. Line
capacities are given with nearly all reels in fishing tackle
catalogues.

Q.34. IF I FISH DIFFERENT WATERS, DO I NEED SEVERAL REELS?

Not necessarily. The counsel of perfection would be to have a
reel for each rod. But if it will hold the right line, a good
medium-sized reel will serve for dry fly and wet fly on any
river, and it won't be too heavy for a brook rod.

Even if you hook a salmon from a boat on a loch, the boat
can usually follow the fish. (I remember a friend of mine
once borrowing a reel and dapping-line from a Scottish
boatman. The line had seen much service. There was a knot
in it every foot or so, and it was about 15 yards long in all,
with no backing. 'Is it-er-long enough?' said my friend.
'No, by God,' said the boatman, 'but I can row like the Devil'.)

A medium-sized reel may let you down badly, however,
when you're attached to a large trout in a reservoir, or perhaps
to a salmon or sea trout in a big river. Then you'd give your
life for something larger, with plenty of backing.

So far as casting is concerned, a long and heavy rod is less
tiring to use if it has a fairly heavy reel. And a brook rod is
more pleasant to use with a light reel. But there is no necessity
to spend money on a vast array of different reels.

Q.35. HOW ABOUT SPARE SPOOLS?

These are invaluable. They represent another way in which
fishing tackle has improved recently. In the old days reels
were difficult to take apart, and spools couldn't be changed.
Indeed the very idea of changing spools hadn't been popular-

ised. The result was that separate reels had to be used for different lines.

Changing spools—and therefore lines—is a simple matter nowadays. A fisherman need only take one reel with him when he goes out in the morning. Then, if he wishes to change from dry fly to wet fly, or perhaps to a heavier line for casting into the wind, all he has to do is to press a catch and change his spool.

Spool-changing has another advantage besides economy. It helps people to cast better—by changing the line to suit different conditions. The bother of carrying several reels used to make this barely worthwhile. But it seems lazy not to take the opportunity when all it entails is carrying a spare spool.

Q.36. HOW MANY SPARE SPOOLS?

No need to overdo it. Most people—except for enterprising reservoir fishermen—still haven't realised the advantages of carrying a spare spool at all.

One spare spool is enough for the majority of fishermen. If you're fishing a dry-fly river, it's useful to have a spare spool with a slightly heavier line than you normally use. This will help you in a strong headwind. And if you're fishing a salmon river at certain times of the year, it may make sense to have a floating line on your reel and a sinking line on the spare spool. Or vice-versa, of course.

Reservoir fishermen *should* ideally carry several lines. Different weights of line (especially shooting heads) will suit different wind conditions. And different *types* of line—floating, slow-sinking, fast-sinking and sink-tip—can all be useful for the different methods they may use in a single day. But even they can usually be cut down to a couple of spare spools or so.

The actual functions of the different types and weights of line are dealt with in the next chapter.

If you're fishing a wet-fly river, or if you're using wet flies from a boat, one line is quite enough. A spare spool isn't necessary. You'll find plenty of people on *any* sort of water who will tell you that one line is quite enough. And they'll catch plenty of fish. But there are also occasions when a choice of lines will help you to fish better.

Types of Reel

Q.37. SHOULD I HAVE A REEL WITH AN 'EXPOSED FLANGE'?

If you fish on a reservoir—quite possibly. Also if you expect big sea trout or salmon.

Conventional reels have a stationary 'cage' and a spool that revolves inside it. (See A below.) But some reels now have a spool with a 'flange' that fits *over* the cage. (See B below.)

Diagram 18

A   B

Type B is usually called an 'exposed flange' reel and its advantage is that you can slow down a running fish by touching the flange with your fingertips. You may be very grateful for it when a big trout or a salmon is stripping your backing off at an alarming speed. However, the device isn't essential, and in any case you have to take care not to let the revolving flange brush against your clothes.

Q.38. ARE 'MULTIPLYING' FLYREELS A GOOD IDEA?

In theory, yes. When you wind an ordinary reel, every turn of the handle makes the drum revolve once. A multiplying reel is 'geared' so that the drum revolves more than once— usually about $2\frac{1}{2}$ times.

So you can reel in faster. This saves time all through a day's fishing. And it's even more helpful when you hook a fish that runs straight towards you—because you can regain contact with him all the more quickly. As against this, multiplying reels have a more complex mechanism. This makes them more expensive and also heavier. And many people find them rather awkward to wind quickly.

All in all, multiplying reels should be of *most* value to those fishermen who use fairly heavy rods in the first place. So far as other fishermen are concerned they constitute an 'optional extra'.

Q.39. ARE AUTOMATIC FLYREELS USEFUL?

In most peoples opinion, no. These reels have never been so popular in this country as they are abroad. They contain a clockwork mechanism which is wound up whenever line is stripped off. When you want to retrieve line, you press a lever conveniently placed near the little finger of your casting hand. The line is wound in by the clockwork. You don't have to turn a handle and the reels don't even possess one. (See diagram below.)

Diagram 19

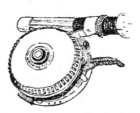

There is nothing wrong with the making of these reels. They are extremely well-made. They retrieve line very quickly, far more quickly than a multiplying reel, and the clockwork has a 'slipping' device to prevent overwinding. But they are very, very heavy.

Apart from their weight, automatic reels need a great deal of getting used to. And even with practice, you don't have the same feeling of control as with a conventional reel. But perhaps their day may come.

Q.40. WHICH TYPE OF REEL SHOULD *I* HAVE?

Unless it's for a reservoir, a perfectly simple and conventional reel is by far the best. There are no extra mechanical devices to add weight. And it will even be adequate for a reservoir, provided it has a large enough line-capacity.

But when fish run very big in open water, a reel with some special 'extra' may land you that fish of a lifetime when others might fail you. And you have a wide choice. You can have an 'exposed flange' reel, giving you rim control. Or you can have a multiplying reel, which adds more weight. Or you can have a multiplying reel *with* an exposed flange. Or you can have a heavy automatic.

Perhaps the best choice of all is just a reel with an exposed flange. It is the lightest and there is less to go wrong.

Q.41. SHOULD ALL REELS HAVE A DRAG?

Most good reels do. With an adjustable drag you can make the line more easy or less easy to pull out, according to the breaking-strength of the leader.

The usual type of adjustable drag is simple enough. It consists of a screw on the rim of the reel which tightens or loosens the pressure of the spring against the pawl. This means that the ratchet-wheel will be either harder or easier to turn. (See Anatomy of a Reel on page 192.)

There are other forms of drag. Some are more complicated and some are found on the side of the reel. They are easier to operate while a fish is being played.

Q.42. SHOULD REELS HAVE INTERCHANGEABLE RIGHT- AND LEFT-HAND WINDS?

Nearly all reels have this feature. If you're left-handed, or if you always use your left hand for winding in, you'll need it. But it won't be because of the advantage of interchangeability. It'll be simply because there aren't any reels specially made for left-handers.

Another advantage of these reels is that they normally provide a spare spring and pawl—the most likely parts to wear out.

Buying a Reel

Q.43. WHAT MAKES SOME REELS SO MUCH MORE EXPENSIVE THAN OTHERS?

As with rods, the most expensive components of reels are *good material and the time of skilled labour.*

A great many reels are made mainly of aluminium alloy. Some alloys are better than others. They are harder, stronger and more resistant to corrosion. They are lighter as well. And they are more expensive. One or two very light reels are now being made of carbon fibre or magnesium alloy.

Skilled labour is needed during the machining process. Modern machines are very accurate but every so often one part of a reel may be a fraction of a centimetre out. This part won't find its way into a first-class reel, because of good supervision and frequent checking. And that always costs money.

A really good reel is a pleasure to own. It's a precision instrument, beautifully smooth in sound and action. Like a rod, it can become an old friend. But this is not to say that inexpensive reels are in the least inefficient.

There aren't nearly so *many* reels on the market as there are rods, and this is fortunate. It means that most reel-makers can take advantage of the economies of mass production.

Many of the less expensive reels, produced in large quantity, are very good indeed. If a fisherman wants to economise on his tackle, he should start with the reel. An inexpensive reel won't harm his casting. He'll catch just as many fish.

Q.44. WHAT ARE THE SIGNS OF A GOOD REEL?

The various components of a reel are shown in the Anatomy of a Reel on page 192. Here are some details that will indicate a reel's quality:

(a) *Cage.* The outer part of the reel is called the 'cage'. It should be well-finished and well-made—from corrosion-resistant aluminium alloy. Any tiny 'craters' in the surface signify that the alloy has been badly cast and is porous. You will seldom find them.

(b) *Drum.* This fits into the cage and is made of the same material. The front-plate should have air holes in it. These let air in to ventilate the line. They also let water out. And they reduce the weight of the reel. On really good reels, there is often a brass bush inside the drum. Some drums revolve around a ball-bearing race. This is unnecessary if the reel has been accurately machined. The fit should be snug. The gap between cage and drum should never be large enough to trap a line. If the reel rattles when you shake it, the drum has not been properly fitted to the spindle. Another test is to press on one side of the spool. If that side yields to the pressure and rubs against the cage when you turn the handle, the reel is badly-made.

(c) *Spindle, ratchet-wheel, spring, pawl.* These should be made of hardened steel. Sometimes a second spring and a second pawl appear opposite the first pair. These can be used either as spares (which are often useful) or for changing from right-hand to left-hand wind. On some reels the change can also be made with a single pawl— by altering the direction in which it points.

(d) *Drag.* Here a screw (sometimes called a 'check') increases or decreases the pressure of the spring on the pawl, making it either harder or easier for the drum to revolve. It should have a milled edge so that your fingers won't slip on it. And the screw should be recessed so that the line won't catch in it. (Some good modern reels have levers instead of screws.)

(e) *Quick-release catch.* This should be easy to operate. If it is, it allows a spool to be changed in a matter of moments. Sometimes there is no quick-release catch, and a screw attaches the front-plate to the reel. A screw used to be considered a sign of a well-made reel—but that was before the development of modern mechanisms. A screw is now old-fashioned, since it slows down spool-changing.

(f) *Line-guard.* A line-guard protects the dressing on the line. It should be made of hard chromed brass, stainless steel or 'German silver'. Many people believe that a line-guard's purpose is to 'guide' the line into the butt-ring. This isn't so. The line-guard stops the line wearing a groove in the side of the reel when line is being stripped off by hand during casting. If a groove does appear, it will scrape dressing from the line.

(g) *Reel-handle.* This should taper *outwards* where it meets the surface of the reel. Alternatively, there should be a small plate between the handle and the reel. Either device will help to avoid strain at the base of the handle.

The handle should turn easily on its screw. Some handles are called 'finger-shaped' because they have grooves to make them easier to hold.

(h) *The sound of a reel.* This is by far the simplest test of a reel's quality. A reel should revolve with a smooth 'purr' rather than an irregular clatter. If it clatters when you strip line off it, the ratchet is too coarse. And if it rattles when it's shaken, the individual parts are badly machined and badly fitted. Look for a better reel.

ANATOMY OF A REEL

Section 3
Lines

Fishing has been described as 'a piece of string with a worm at one end and a fool at the other'. This section concerns itself with the pieces of string used for flyfishing.

Lines are more crucial to flyfishing than to any other fishing method. The introduction of suitable lines for casting—i.e. tapered lines—came about a hundred years ago. Yet some fishermen are still totally unaware that the weight and taper of a line are as important to good casting as the weight and taper of a rod. The incorrect matching of rod and line is one of the most frequent reasons for poor casting. Correct matching can improve almost anyone's performance out of all recognition.

Tapers

Q.45. WHY SHOULD A LINE BE TAPERED AT ALL?

To make it go out satisfactorily. The fisherman transmits energy *through* a rod *into* a line. The energy is transferred from the rod to the line at the point where they meet. That is, at the very tip of the rod.

If the line is fairly thick at this point, its weight will give it plenty of momentum. So far, so good. But if it continues to be thick all the way down, the momentum will die away very quickly. Far better for the thickness to taper off gradually. Then the energy flows easily all down the length of the line, right to the very tip.

Here's a demonstration. Tie one end of a piece of string to a big stone and the other to a little stone. If you throw the big stone, it will carry the little stone with it through the air. But however hard you throw the little stone, it won't budge the big one. That's why a line should be thick at the rod-tip and thin at the end.

And tapered lines have other advantages:

(a) *More line-speed.* The thick part of the line transfers its *speed* to the thin part, as well as its energy. The whole line travels faster. And longer casts are made possible.

(b) *Less air-resistance.* The last few yards of a tapered line have only a small diameter and offer little air-resistance.

So the tip 'turns over' more easily, even against a wind.

  (c) *Delicacy.* A thin line-tip lands more lightly on the water.

Q.46. ARE 'LEVEL' LINES OUT-OF-DATE?

Not quite. They have the advantage of being easier to make than tapered lines, and are therefore cheaper. When it isn't necessary to cast particularly carefully—and (no offence) boat fishermen on many lochs don't have to when the wind's behind—a level line is effective enough. But whenever good casting matters, level lines are hopelessly inadequate.

Q.47. HOW MANY SORTS OF TAPER ARE THERE?

In a sense there's really only one *sort* of taper. When they're being used for casting *all* tapered lines are thickest at (or very near) the rod-tip. And they're thinnest at the end. But none of them have regular and 'continuous' tapers. There are in fact three main types of tapered line.

These three types are shown in the Anatomy of a Line on page 205. When you look at them, remember that only the front 30 feet or 40 feet will be beyond the rod-tip while you're false-casting.

  (a) *Double-taper lines.* These lines are usually 30 yards long in all. They have a long 'belly' in the middle and a taper at either end. Only one of those tapers is used at any one time for casting. The other is simply there so that the line can be reversed and enjoy a 'second life' when one end becomes too worn.

  (b) *Forward-taper lines.* Also called 'weight-forward' or 'torpedo' lines. Again, these lines are usually 30 yards long. Only one end is *ever* used for casting. The weight of the line is concentrated beyond the rod-tip. The belly is relatively short. There is a front taper as usual. But behind the belly is a very short back taper and a long stretch of fine 'shooting line' which travels easily through the rings on the final cast.

(c) *Shooting Heads*. In effect a shooting head is simply the front (or back) 30 feet of a double-taper line. At its butt it stops abruptly and is attached to backing or 'shooting line'. This will consist of monofilament or braided line or of a special, very thin, floating line. There is a small loop at the butt-end of some shooting heads so that the backing can be easily tied on. Another name for this backing or shooting line is 'running line'.

Q.48. HOW DO THESE TAPERS AFFECT CASTING?

The big difference lies in the varying amounts of line that you can shoot with your final cast.

Imagine that you are using a double taper line and that you're false-casting with about 30 feet to 40 feet of it beyond the rod tip. When you eventually make your final cast, you'll be able to shoot a little line—but not very much. Double-taper lines are poor shooters because the 'casting line' always has to pull out *heavy* line behind it. And it's not only a question of weight, but of added friction and air-resistance as well.

Applying the same principles, a forward-taper line will shoot farther—since it has thinner and lighter line behind it. And a shooting head, which only has to draw out very fine line or monofilament, will shoot farthest of all.

Q.49 WHEN SHOULD I USE A DOUBLE-TAPER LINE?

A double-taper line has three assets:

(a) *Long life*. A double-taper line is the only kind that can be reversed.

(b) *Delicacy*. Double-taper lines may shoot badly. But there's a compensating advantage. The force of a cast is 'dampened' more gradually. This helps delicacy, particularly so when the wind is behind. The cast is less likely to end abruptly. And that makes it rather easier to set the fly down lightly.

(c) *Aerialisation*. It is difficult to aerialise more than 35 feet of a *forward-taper* line without losing control. The thick part of the line gets too far away from the rod-tip. But if a caster does want to aerialise more line, he can do so with a *double-taper* because it has a longer belly.

Q.50.   WHEN SHOULD I USE A FORWARD-TAPER LINE?

A forward-taper line has two great advantages:

(a) *Distance.* You can shoot a good deal of line with a forward taper, and so cast farther than you could with a double-taper.

(b) *Casting into the wind.* Because it shoots better, and because the thin shooting line offers little air resistance, a forward-taper goes out well into a wind. And the tip 'turns over' quickly—before the wind can blow it back.

Q.51.   HOW ABOUT A SHOOTING HEAD?

You can *aerialise* least line of all with a shooting head, since usually there are only 30 feet of it altogether. To achieve distance, you have to shoot a great deal of backing through the rings. And so you can, to cast a very long way indeed—though it takes a lot of practice to present a fly really well, without splash, with a shooting head.

(a) *Reservoir fishermen.* Shooting heads have found an ideal role in the hands of reservoir fishermen. If they wade a little into the water, they can use the surface of the water itself for laying out their shooting line ready to cast. Or they can use 'line-rafts' and 'stripping baskets' of various kinds.

(b) *Professional casters.* Shooting heads were first invented by two tournament casters in 1946. Their team won the tournament. Ever since then, tournament casters have been beating previous records with the help of shooting heads. They sometimes have a routine whereby an assistant takes care of the shooting line.

Distance casting with a shooting head calls for the 'double-haul' technique. Again this puts the reservoir fisherman at an advantage because 'double-hauling' is something he often learns. (It is quite unnecessary for dry-fly fishing on rivers.)

Q.52. IS A SHOOTING HEAD ALWAYS 30 FEET?

Not always. Ready-made shooting heads are invariably 30 feet long, so that even a near-beginner can aerialise them without too much difficulty. But most experienced fishermen find they can aerialise rather more than this, and so gain some extra distance.

If you want a shooting head to match you and your rod perfectly, it's very, very easy to make one. Simply get a double-tapered line (or, better still, half a line) of the weight you want, and see how much of it you can aerialise consistently, without too much effort. Then cut it off at the rod-tip, splice or needle-knot it to your backing or shooting line, and you have your own tailor-made shooting head.

Here's one important thing to remember. For every 6 feet you add to the standard 30 feet, you are effectively adding to the aerialised weight by one AFTM number. (See Question 54.) This means that if your rod is rated to cast 30 feet of AFTM 8 line, a 36-foot shooting head should be made up from AFTM 7 line. Longer-than-usual shooting heads are perhaps best when made of floating line, since it's awkward to 'pick up' a long length of sinking line from the water.

If you use a monofilament backing, it should be about 20–30 lb. breaking strain. This is stiff enough not to tangle, but not *so* stiff and wiry that its coils won't shoot easily.

Weight of Line

Q.53. WHY IS THE WEIGHT OF A LINE SO IMPORTANT?

Because it *must* match the rod. This can't be over-emphasized. It is vital to good casting. If a line is too light, it won't flex the rod properly. So the rod can't gather power, and can't deliver any. And if the line's too heavy, the rod will only be able to aerialise a very short length before straining or breaking.

Q.54. HOW DO I KNOW THE WEIGHT OF A LINE?

Any line you buy will have the weight marked on the box or package. It may have the *size* marked as well. These two properties of a line—weight and size—should never be confused.

(a) *Size.* At one time lines were classified mainly by size. Different letters of the alphabet (A, B, C, etc.) were allotted to different diameters (see chart below). The biggest line was an A.

CHART I

Line Size Equivalents

Designation	Inches	Millimetres
A	·060	1·50
B	·055	1·40
C	·050	1·27
D	·045	1·15
E	·040	1·00
F	·035	0·89
G	·030	0·76
H	·025	0·64
I	·022	0·56

If a line were designated HEH, therefore, it was bound to be a double-taper line. Each tip would be about 0·64 mm. and the belly about 1·0 mm. An HDG would be a forward-taper or weight-forward line, with a shooting line of 0·76 mm., a belly of 1·15 mm. and a tip of 0·64 mm. Since nearly all lines used to be made of the same material—braided silk—it could be assumed that if two different makes of line possessed identical diameters, their weights would also be identical. But then plastic lines were invented. Their weight/diameter ratios were quite different. It soon became clear that a new designation for lines had to be found.

(b) *Weight.* The standard designation for lines now follows the AFTM scale. AFTM stands for Association of Fishing Tackle Manufacturers and their scale consists of a series of numbers from 1 to 12. These numbers indicate the *weight* of a line regardless of diameter, No. 1 being the lightest and No. 12 being the heaviest.

The AFTM scale classifies a line according to the weight of *the first* 30 feet (excluding the level tip). This length was chosen as the usual amount of line aerialised.

You will find an AFTM number on the packaging of every line. Sometimes the *size* (HEH, etc.) is given as well. This can be useful information, particularly in determining the right taper for a leader, but it is now secondary.

Q.55. WHAT DOES WF-5-S MEAN?

This *isn't* an alternative nomenclature. It's used to give *additional* information about a line, as follows:

(a) The first letter or two letters indicate the taper. L stands for level. DT stands for double-taper. WF stands for weight-forward. ST stands for shooting taper. So the line above is a weight-forward.

(b) Next comes the AFTM number, indicating the weight of the first thirty feet. In this case the line is a No. 5.

(c) Finally, there is a single letter—F for a floating line or S for a sinking line. If a line can either float or sink, according to whether it's greased or not, the letter I for Intermediate appears. The line in question is a weight-forward No. 5 sinking line.

Similarly, 'DT-6-F' would designate a double-taper No. 6 floating line.

Q.56. HOW DO I MATCH A LINE TO MY ROD?

If you buy a new rod you're almost bound to find an AFTM number marked on the butt, near the maker's name. This number gives the weight of line which the maker recommends for the rod. The practice of indicating the right line on a rod is a fairly recent one, and it is a great help.

It's worth bearing in mind, however, that the recommended line will be for 'average' casters. The *best* line for a rod varies with each individual's experience, and with the power he puts into his casting.

(a) *Beginners.* People who haven't done much casting can seldom aerialise much line. They won't have mastered the rhythm of the exercise. Their casting muscles will still be unused to it. They'll only be able to get out a short length of line, without much weight in it. There may not be enough weight to flex the rod, so the rod can't deliver any power for them.

This is a very common occurrence. And it's a pity. The beginner starts with the disadvantage of only being able to put a minimal amount of power into the rod. Then the rod seems to fail him utterly, He makes no progress and he can't understand it. *Answer*: he should use a line one AFTM number *heavier* than the one recommended.

(b) *Average fishermen.* These are the people for whom the recommended line should be just right. It usually is. But if they are not used to casting over 30 feet, or if their fishing only calls for short casting, they too may do better with a heavier line. (They should easily be able to tell whether or not their rod is flexing as fully as it should.) They may also find a heavier line useful for the occasional task of casting on tricky days into a bad head-wind.

(c) *Very good casters.* These can often use a line *lighter* than the recommended one. This is because they can aerialise *more* than the average amount of line, and put more power behind their casting. They could even strain the rod with an 'average' line. So they should step their line down by one AFTM number for very long distances.

(d) *Reservoir fishermen.* A number of reservoir rods can handle two or three weights of shooting head. The more difficult the wind, the heavier should be the shooting head.

You may come by a rod with no AFTM number on it. It may be a second-hand rod. Or you may have inherited it. If you're uncertain which weight of line to buy for it, it's well worth asking an experienced fisherman. Show him your rod or tell him the name of it. And tell him also the sort of distance you expect to be casting.

Q.57. DO YOU RECOMMEND CUTTING THE TIP OF A LINE?

Hardly ever. Some people have found that their leader and fly 'turn over' better when they shorten a line by cutting a few inches of the tip. But be careful—the value of this varies a great deal with the person *and* with the make of line. Once you've cut some inches off, you can't tie them back on.

So if you think that your leader and fly turn over badly, make quite sure that nothing else is wrong. *First* check that your own casting isn't at fault. See how a competent friend casts with the same tackle. *Next* see if your leader matches the line. If there's too much difference in diameter between the tip of the line and the butt of the leader, this could be the cause. Only then—and it will be a rare occasion—need you even consider taking a pair of scissors to your line.

Types of Line

Q.58. WHAT IS SO 'REVOLUTIONARY' ABOUT PLASTIC LINES?

All flylines used to be made of silk until the 'revolution' caused by the introduction of plastic lines. Silk is still the only alternative and at the moment silk lines are virtually unobtainable. But at least one manufacturer is trying to revive them, so I'll talk about them here as if they were easy to get. The two types of line are made on rather different principles.

(a) *Silk.* These lines are braided from pure silk. The tapers are 'built-in' during the braiding. They are then treated or 'dressed' with linseed oil and painstakingly hand-polished to give them buoyancy and resistance to water-absorption. They float when greased and sink when ungreased.

(b) *Plastic.* Plastic lines have a more complicated dual construction. They have a braided nylon 'core'. But their real secret lies in the plastic dressing. This can have a specific gravity which is lighter than water, so that the line floats without greasing. Or the specific gravity can be heavier than water, so that the line sinks.   Again, the specific gravity can be varied to make a line float for most of its length, and sink for the rest. Then it's an F/S line.

(c) *Other materials.* Some braided lines are made on the same principle as silk lines but are braided from terylene or similar materials. Their reputation has never been as high as that of plastic or silk lines.

Q.59. WHAT ARE THE ADVANTAGES OF PLASTIC LINES?

So far as the floating lines are concerned, it's probable that *most* people buy them simply because they can't be bothered to grease a silk line. But plastic lines have many other merits.

(a) The dressing is *smoother* than that of a silk line. This helps them to shoot farther.

(b) They need less maintenance than silk lines. They can be left on the reel after fishing without any danger. Silk lines perish quickly unless they are stripped off to dry after use.

(c) Plastic sinking lines can be made so that they sink either quickly or slowly. The fast-sinking varieties will get a fly deep down very soon, if that is where the trout are feeding.

(d) The floating lines (but not the sinking ones) are bulkier than silk lines of the same weight. It is possible to cast farther with them—even without shooting—if the wind is *behind*.

Q.60. THEN WHY USE A SILK LINE?

Some fishermen have always preferred them, especially dry-fly fishermen. Silk lines have no obvious advantages for the wet fly, except that they can always be greased to serve double-duty for dry-fly as well. But a dry-fly man can find a great deal to like about them, two things in particular:

(a) *Diameter.* Silk lines are less bulky than plastic floating lines, which have to be relatively thick in order to accommodate their 'millions of air cells'. So a silk line offers less air resistance and—if shooting qualities are disregarded—will carry better into a wind.

(b) *Delicacy*. The *tip* of a silk line can be far finer than that of a plastic line. The dual construction of the latter won't allow too fine a tip. This means that a silk line can be matched to a leader with a thinner butt, and they will both fall lightly on the water.

Q.61. ARE PLASTIC FLOATING LINES FOR DRY-FLY FISHING *ONLY*?

No. There are several aspects of floating lines which are not so well-known as they should be. Many people may also have been misled by advertisements implying that these lines float all day and *never* sink. This isn't quite true.

(a) *Scum*. A floating line will sink if it gets scum or algae on it. Some rivers and still waters often collect scum in the surface-film. If your line sinks then, it's not a faulty one. Simply wipe it clean and it will float again.

(b) *The tip*. The last 18–22 inches of most floating lines *never* float properly. They either lie 'awash' or else sink a little. So if you're dry-fly fishing and definitely want *all* the line to float, you should grease the tip. (Do *not* use silicone grease, which affects the dressing.)

The sinking tip of a floating line is an asset in two ways. It makes the floating line more useful for wet-fly and nymph fishing. And on reservoirs you can sink the fly as deep as your leader is long, provided you retrieve it slowly.

Q.62. WHICH TYPE OF LINE MAKES THE BEST SHOOTING HEAD?

A sinking plastic line is the most popular type. It dominates the sales of ready-made shooting heads. For its weight it has an even smaller diameter than a silk line, and a far smaller diameter than a floating line. So it shoots farthest of all, even into a wind.

If you want a shooting head which floats, you might make

one from a double-taper silk line. It will shoot reasonably well
—because the whole of it will be beyond the rod-tip while
you're false-casting. And it won't have so large a diameter as a
plastic floating line.

Q.63. DO PLASTIC LINES NEED ANY SPECIAL CARE?

Plastic lines are extremely easy to maintain. But if they are
misused the dressing sometimes cracks. The two commonest
misuses are:

(a) *Bad casting.* Some people make an audible whip-like
'crack' while they're casting. Whenever this happens, the
line-dressing is likely to crack too. The mistake being
made is that of starting a forward cast too soon, and it
should be avoided at all costs.

(b) *Petroleum derivatives.* If a line comes into contact with a
petroleum derivative, the dressing may be harmed.
Petroleum derivatives include oil, oily water (in boats
with outboard engines), suntan oil, some insect repellents
—and silicone floatants.

Q.64. WHAT IS THE BEST COLOUR FOR A LINE?

Once more, it depends on the sort of flyfishing you do.

(a) *Dry fly.* White is the commonly accepted colour for a dry-
fly line, and the vast majority of dry-fly fishermen use it.
The idea is that if a trout catches sight of it, he'll see it
against the light background of the sky and therefore
won't be able to make it out very well. But for reasons
rather too complicated to explain, a small but growing
number of fishermen, of whom I am one, now prefer a dark
colour (such as mahogany) for their floating line. This
applies particularly to stillwater fishing—because on a
river the trout should never see the line anyway.

(b) *Sunk fly.* White lines will serve for fishing a shallow downstream wet fly, because the trout will see the fly before he
sees the line. But if you are fishing really deep, or if you are

fishing a reservoir or loch, green or brown lines are better. They are less visible against any *dark* background.

Q.65. WHAT SHOULD I LOOK FOR IN BUYING A LINE?

There are few outward signs of a line's quality. The durability of the dressing can only be proved in use. And you cannot measure the taper unless you carry a micrometer. If you buy a plastic line, examine the dressing to see that it is sheer and smooth. It should have no roughness, let alone any cracks. And satisfy yourself also that the line is supple. This is important. If it is too wiry, the coils will not shoot well.

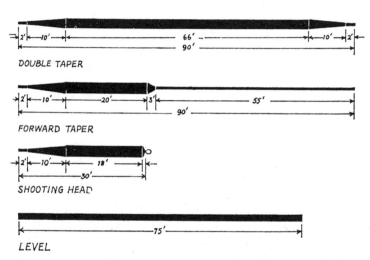

DOUBLE TAPER

FORWARD TAPER

SHOOTING HEAD

LEVEL

THE ANATOMY OF A LINE

Q.66. HOW IMPORTANT IS BACKING?

More important than most people think. Backing has two functions:

(a) It fills out the spool, so that your retrieval rate is as fast as possible when you reel in. Always make sure your spool is nearly full—to just below the brim. If it isn't, you will retrieve too little line every time you turn the handle. (If it's *completely* full, however, the line may start overlapping the brim while it's being wound in—with a consequent risk of tangling.)

(b) It enables a large fish to run a long way. This is vital on reservoirs.

So it is not worth using 'any old stuff' for backing. Get good monofilament or shooting line to back shooting heads. And for other flylines use standard man-made backing. It's not expensive, and it won't rot. Then it only remains to make sure that it's properly joined to the line.

Section 4
Presentation, Leaders and Sundries

This appendix is about tackle. It isn't a 'How to Catch Trout' appendix. But tackle that 'presents' the fly properly is very important to the catching of trout. 'Presentation' is the art of making line, leader and fly fall very lightly on the water, all in a straight line. So long as they fall lightly, the trout won't be scared out of their wits. And if they fall in a straight line the fly will start fishing immediately.

It is extremely difficult to achieve delicate presentation with a very long cast. A few experts can land their fly lightly on a spot far away, but most mortals can't. When you cast your maximum distance, you are almost certain to present the fly *less* than perfectly.

So you frequently have to choose between distance and good presentation. Sometimes your longest cast will catch a fish that you wouldn't otherwise have found. But it is also true that more big fish are caught *within* a range of 15 yards than outside it, even on reservoirs. Better presentation plays its part in this.

The right tackle—which includes a well-matched leader to suit a well-matched rod and line—is an immense aid to good presentation.

Q.67. HOW DOES THE LEADER HELP IN PRESENTATION?

The commonest tragedy in casting is when the line lands on the water satisfactorily, but when the leader and fly fall in an untidy heap just beyond it. Apart from bad casting there are two frequent reasons for it:

(a) *Mis-matching of leader*. The leader may not have been correctly matched to the line. A modern plastic line is bulkier at its tip than a silk line is. The butt of the leader should be thick enough to continue the taper smoothly.

(b) *Poor turn-over*. The end of the leader may not have 'turned over'. To a large extent it's the job of the caster and his rod to make it do so, but the leader can be at fault too. **If its tip is too thin and limp, the air resistance of the fly may stop it turning over. This applies particularly to dry** flies, and a large bushy fly like a Mayfly certainly needs a leader with a stiff tip.

Q.68. HOW DO I CHOOSE THE RIGHT LEADER?

It's best to make up your leaders yourself from varying weights of nylon, since then you can match them perfectly to your line and fly.

(a) *Butt*. The butt of your leader should usually be a little thicker than those of most ready-made leaders. Only in the case of silk lines with thin tips can the butt of the leader afford to be thin too.

A good rule-of-thumb is that the diameter of the leader-butt should be at least half that of the line-tip. The diameters of different lines are given on page 198. Some 'average' nylon diameters are shown overleaf.

(b) *Tip*. Many people use a tip as fine as they dare, in the hope of deceiving gut-shy trout. But the gut-shyness of trout isn't the only consideration. It is sometimes even more important to match the tip to the *size of the fly*. Large dry flies make *thin* tips turn over badly. A big Mayfly needs a tip of at least 0·22 mm. or 5¼ lb. breaking-strain. *Small* dry flies, on the other hand, land and float

CHART 2

Nylon Diameter/Strengths

Diameter in inches	Diameter in millimetres	Breaking-strain in lb.	X equivalent
·0031	0·08	$\frac{3}{4}$	
·0039	0·10	$1\frac{1}{4}$	
·0047	0·12	$1\frac{3}{4}$	7x
·0055	0·14	2	6x
·0063	0·16	$2\frac{1}{2}$	5x
·0071	0·18	$3\frac{3}{4}$	4x
·0079	0·20	4	3x
·0087	0·22	$5\frac{1}{4}$	2x
·0094	0·24	$6\frac{1}{4}$	1x
·0102	0·26	7	0x
·0110	0·28	8	
·0118	0·30	$9\frac{1}{2}$	
·0138	0·35	$12\frac{1}{4}$	
·0158	0·40	$16\frac{1}{2}$	
·0178	0·45	$20\frac{3}{4}$	
·0198	0·50	$25\frac{1}{2}$	

awkwardly with thick tips. A diminutive black gnat should be fished with a tip no bigger than 0·18 mm. or $3\frac{3}{4}$ lb. breaking-strain—unless extremely big fish are expected.

Wet flies and nymphs do not present nearly so much air resistance, but the same rules still apply. The large hooks of big flies can't be driven home by very thin tips. And small flies swim badly on tips that are too thick.

(c) *Taper.* A continuous taper is *not* ideal for a leader. It will turn over better if most of its weight is towards the butt. A good leader should have a long, level butt. It should then taper fairly steeply into the tip.

(d) *Knots.* The breaking-strains given for nylon don't take knots into account. Any knot reduces the breaking-strain. Even a good knot reduces it by 20 per cent. A bad one will do so far more. Always use the knots specially recommended for nylon. See Appendix B.

Q.69. WHAT'S THE BEST WAY OF JUDGING
        FLIES?

Flies vary a great deal. It's useful to be able to tell good tyings
from bad tyings. Dry flies are the most difficult to tie, which is
why good ones are often expensive. Here are some means of
assessing them:

(a) *Do the hackles cover the point of the hook?* If so, the fly is badly
tied. Hackles over the hook may not affect the hooking
of fish to any great extent, but they overbalance the fly so
that it tilts forward unnaturally when it's floating.

(b) *Have the hackles been clipped?* It is easy to see when hackles
have been clipped, because the ends will all be level and
thicker than usual. Fly-tyers sometimes clip hackles to
render them stiffer and to make the fly float better. It
only shows that the hackles weren't top-quality in the
first place. Clipped hackles make indentations in the
surface-film of the water which are too large for a natural
fly.

(c) *Has the fly been neatly finished near the eye?* The area round
the eye should be neatly varnished and shouldn't show
stray ends of tying material. There should be no varnish
in the eye itself.

(d) *Will the fly sit up on a table?* A good fly will sit upright on
any flat surface. If it topples over sideways on a table, it
may do so on the water.

As regards wet flies, only point (c) applies. But there are two
other questions to ask about them:

(a) *Are the hackles streamlined?* Wet-fly hackles should never
stick out from the body. If they do, the fly will travel
through the water unrealistically. Most underwater
creatures are streamlined.

(b) *Are the wings straight?* The wings should sweep back
straight over the top of the body. The fly will swim
lopsidedly if the wings aren't central.

Q.70. ANYTHING TO SAY ABOUT BAGS AND
        NETS?

There are plenty of bags on the market, many of them very

practical. You can choose the one you like best. A bad bag is
unlikely to lose you a fish. But a bad net can lose you several in
a day.

The best nets, unfortunately, are the least convenient to carry
about. A good net should have a fixed, rigid head. This helps
you to 'feel' for a fish in the weeds. And it unfolds easily when
you want it.

This isn't so true of 'collapsible' nets with triangular frames.
They may be simpler to pack and carry, but they have a habit
of getting entangled in their own meshes when you need them
most. Then nothing will induce them to unfold. And they are
useless in weed.

If you want convenience in a net, you must pay for it in
efficiency. Your net—whichever type it is—should ideally have
a 'locking head'. This keeps the frame in position once it's been
unfolded. A long handle is useful for boat fishing or for landing
a fish from a high bank, but it can be awkward when clipped to
a bag. It's too easy to stumble over. Telescopic handles resolve
this particular dilemma.

A net should be large enough for big fish. But the mesh itself
should never be too wide, since you may want to land under-
sized fish before you return them. If they slip through the mesh
they may damage themselves.

Q.71.   WHICH ARE THE BEST WADERS?

You may on very rare occasions need chest-waders. But thigh-
waders are usually quite sufficient for trout fishing.

There are two points worth remembering about waders:

(a) *Are they slip-proof*? Rubber soles are dangerous,unless they
are used only in silt or fine gravel. Studs slip least on wet
grass. But felt—since it has a larger gripping surface—is
best on rocks. Studded heels and felt soles are perhaps the
ideal, but studded heels *and* soles are usually perfectly
safe.

(b) *Are they reinforced*? Good waders should be reinforced on
the inside of each knee. This is where they wear first if
they're constantly used and aren't reinforced. (In storage
they will wear wherever they're made to stay creased.)

Q.72. ANY ADVICE ON FISHING COATS?

A good fishing coat should be long enough to overlap the tops of thigh-waders, and also long enough to cover a fisherman's seat when he sits down on a damp bank.

It is important that all the seams should be sealed inside. Otherwise water will come through the holes made by the stitching.

As regards material, only plastic is *completely* waterproof. But some other good materials are so nearly waterproof that it makes little difference. They will keep out the wet very efficiently—except perhaps a whole day's downpour.

All waterproof materials cause condensation on the *inside*. So don't always blame the coat if you find it's a little damp there.

Q.73. HOW ABOUT FLYBOXES, ETC?

They aren't really within our scope. Ample information about flyboxes, spring balances, priests—and other fishing accessories—is easy enough to come by. They are excellently described and illustrated in many fishing tackle catalogues and fishing books. The object of this appendix has been to concentrate on the aspects of tackle that aren't usually explained.

Q.74. DOES FLY TACKLE NEED A LOT OF CARE?

Modern tackle needs remarkably little attention during the season. The little care it requires takes far less time than, say, cleaning a gun—and it is well worthwhile.

(a) *Rod.* Cane rods should be wiped dry. They should never be left in a damp rod-bag. Glass rods are less affected by damp, but they should also be wiped dry. Keep both cane and glass rods in a cool, dry place—hanging them up by the loop on the rod-bag. Don't lace up the rod-bag too tightly. Never keep cane rods for a long period of time in a closed metal or plastic tube. They may suffer if the air cannot get at them.

(b) *Reel.* A good reel, if it's been lightly oiled at the beginning of the season, will not need re-oiling for some time. Nor should it be harmed by a little damp. Nevertheless, it's only wise to dry a reel if it is soaking wet. If the drum is

taken out of the cage, dry air will reach the working parts
more easily.

(c) *Line*. Today's plastic lines do not need drying. They can
be left on the reel. Silk lines should be stripped off and
left to dry.

(d) *Waders*. Waders should never be left damp longer than
necessary. But careless drying can do them harm. They
should not be dried in front of direct heat. The rubber
will perish quickly. Waders will dry soon if the air of a
warm house can reach inside them. If possible they
should be hung up by the feet to avoid creasing. Various
types of 'wader hanger' are available.

At the end of the season, it's a good idea to make sure that
your tackle will be in good order when trout fishing comes
round again. The whole process takes only a few minutes.

(a) *Rod*. Give it the end-of-a-day treatment already described. Before storing it, inspect it carefully to see
whether it needs overhauling. Make sure that the pro-
tective varnish (if any) hasn't cracked anywhere. Check
the tyings of all rod-rings and inspect them for wear,
especially the butt- and tip-rings. Lightly oil the screws
and rings of screw-grip reel-fittings. Check that the
ferrules are clean. Male ferrules can be lubricated with
the stub of a candle. (Never use vaseline or oil on ferrules,
only tallow or candlewax.)

(b) *Reel*. Take the drum from the cage, clean and oil lightly
before storing. Take care that oil does not spill on the
line. Check that the line has not worn a groove in the
line-guard or in the side of the reel.

(c) *Line*. Make sure that line *and* backing are dry before they
are stored. Check the splice between line and backing.
Silk lines should be stored in loose coils *off* the reel.

(d) *Waders*. If waders are not to be worn for several months,
it is even more important to hang them up by the feet.

(e) *Nylon*. It is safest to replace nylon each season. The out-
lay is not immense. But if you wish to store it, make sure
it's in the dark. Nothing destroys nylon more quickly

than strong light—especially sunshine. (For this reason, never buy nylon that's 'on view' in a shop window.)

(f) *Flies.* If you're unlucky enough to have a moth problem, keep flies in a mothproof box. Or put camphor with them.

If any of your tackle needs overhauling or repair by a dealer, try to have it done as early as possible in the close-season. Many people leave it till the last minute. Then they may find irritating blockages and delays because dealers are so busy.

I very much hope that you have been able to find in this appendix a few things about tackle which aren't generally known. Good tackle is important. It will complement your own skill. It is almost bound to make your catches just a fraction heavier. It can never promise you good fishing, but it can guarantee that you won't be handicapped by anything except, perhaps, yourself.

Don't let's overestimate it, however. Your own enjoyment is the main thing—whatever tackle you use. And a little knowledge about trout is far more important than having the latest tackle.

APPENDIX B

Knots

Knots, like so many other things in fishing, should be demonstrated rather than written about. Once you have seen someone tie a particular knot, and watched where his fingers and thumbs go in the process, the knot seems far easier than it ever does on paper.

But the diagrams overleaf may help. They represent the knots that are most useful and reliable for nylon.

FIGURE OF EIGHT KNOT
For joining line to loop of leader

Pull tight

HALF BLOOD KNOT
For attaching fly to leader

Pull tight and cut off loose end

DOUBLE TURLE KNOT
**Alternative knot for attaching fly—particularly
when nylon is far finer than the eye of hook**

Pass fly through loops.
draw tight and
cut off loose end

FOUR-TURN BLOOD KNOT
For joining lengths of nylon or making droppers

To make a dropper leave one end long   Draw tight and cut off loose ends

NEEDLE KNOT

**For attaching flyline to leader,
or to nylon backing**

1

Pierce line with needle or pin.
Point nylon (with scissors or razor-
blade) and thread through

2

Wind nylon round line 4 or 5
times, Bring end back and lay
alongside

3

Take turn of nylon back over itself

4

Continue until all original turns
are over the end of nylon

5

Pull hard on both ends of nylon,
and finally on end entering line.
Cut off loose end. Varnish if desired

UNIVERSAL OR GRINNER KNOT

A.   For attaching fly to leader

Draw tight and cut off loose end

B.   For making a loop in nylon

Draw tight and cut off loose end

C.   For joining lengths of nylon and making droppers

Draw tight and cut off loose ends. OR leave one end long (the end farthest from line)
to make a dropper

APPENDIX C

Recipes

The most fitting end for a trout is on the table of the man who manages to catch him. I have always felt sorry for fishermen who do not fancy the taste of trout, for they must miss a lot of pleasure—not only in the eating of their trout, but also in the catching of them. There is certainly a sense of added excitement when you land a trout that is needed for a meal. Part of it comes, I suppose, from pure atavism. Or, on more practical grounds, you may feel that you have saved money on the housekeeping bills.

Anyway, the dieticians say that trout are extremely nourishing. Their flesh is usually whiteish. But if they have lived in rivers or lakes where they can eat plenty of shrimps, snails, crayfish or other crustaceans, their flesh becomes beautifully pink. Some trout are as pink as salmon, and this makes them all the more delicious.

Here are a few recipes. At this point, I must acknowledge a great debt of gratitude—to Madame Prunier, of the famous St. James's Street restaurant which bore her name. She very kindly gave me her advice on how to cook trout. No advice could be better.

TO CLEAN A TROUT

Slit the abdomen. Draw out all the entrails, and wash well. Take care, also, to scrape off the thick, dark blood which lies along the backbone of a trout. If left in, this gives the fish a peculiar taste. *Trout should be served whole whenever possible*—since then they look their best. And there is some very good eating under the gills. But if they will not fit into the dish or pan, the heads and tails can be cut off.

FRYING

FRIED TROUT

Clean the fish. Heat some butter in a frying pan. Roll the trout in flour and when the butter is sizzling hot, fry them for five minutes on each side. Sprinkle a little salt on them, and place them on a heated dish with slices of lemon. Serve with a little melted butter, or with a *maitre d'hotel* sauce.

(If the trout weigh half a pound or more, it is usually best to split them before cooking. Simply cut them down the middle, from the inside, so that the two halves open out flat. Then remove the backbone. When the occasion does not demand perfection, however, the backbone can be left in—to be removed at table by whoever eats the trout. Do not fry split trout over too fierce a heat. They may crinkle up, and become hard. Another point—butter is always best for frying trout. If there is not enough butter, other forms of fat will do. But take care to see that the fat is hot enough—just smoking in the case of ordinary cooking fat—before putting in the trout).

SCOTCH TROUT

Proceed exactly as above. Instead of rolling the trout in flour, however, roll them in oatmeal with a sprinkling of salt and pepper. Serve, again, with a little melted butter, or with a *maitre d'hotel* sauce.

TRUITES À LA MEUNIERE
(from Madame Prunier's Fish Cookery Book)

Clean and wipe the trout. Season them, roll them in flour, and cook them in a frying-pan in clarified butter. Arrange them on the serving-dish, scatter chopped parsley over them, sprinkle them lightly with lemon juice, and pour over some butter cooked *à la noisette*. This is butter cooked in a frying pan until it browns slightly and begins to smell of nuts.

(NOTE—It should be observed that cooking fish *à la meunière*, simple as it sounds, needs some care. Too great a heat will brown the skin and the appearance and flavour of the fish will be spoiled. If the cooking is too slow, the fish get soft. Fish properly cooked in this way should be a beautiful golden brown).

TRUITES AMANDE

Fry the cleaned trout gently without flour. When they are half-cooked, scatter some split blanched almonds into the fat. Continue cooking till both trout and almonds are golden-brown. Serve with the almonds arranged round the trout.

GRILLING

GRILLED TROUT

Clean the trout and dry it with a cloth. If the trout is not to be split, make two or three diagonal incisions along each flank with a knife, to hasten cooking. Brush the fish with melted butter. Heat the grill, grease the grid and lay the trout on it. Cook one side till brown, then the other side. Serve with lettuce, water-cress, sliced lemon and melted butter.

Large trout, again, can be split. Cook the skin side briefly first, then finish off with the flesh next to the heat. Rainbow trout are said not to require any butter when being grilled, since they possess more oil than brown trout.

BOILING

BOILED TROUT

Clean the fish. Bring some water to the boil, with salt and plenty of vinegar in it. Draw the water to the edge of the heat, and put in the trout. The water should not boil again, or the flesh of the fish will break up. Cook just below simmering point for about quarter of an hour—perhaps a little less, perhaps a little more, according to the size of the trout. Scatter with parsley. Serve separately melted butter and steamed or boiled potatoes.

TRUITES AU BLEU

The recipe is as above. But, as Madame Prunier says, the essential condition for *truites au Bleu*, cooked properly, is that the fish should be alive. Each trout should be stunned, cleaned as quickly as possible, and plunged immediately into the water. As a result, this dish may not be practicable for most fishermen and many, perhaps, will not like the fact that the trout have to be cooked alive.

TRUITES AU COURT-BOUILLON

Prepare a *court-bouillon*. ᛫This is done in the following way. Pour equal amounts of water and wine vinegar (or white wine if you can afford it) into a pan. There should be enough to cover the trout, which is *not* put in yet. Add salt, pepper, two cloves, a sliced onion, a sliced carrot, and a *bouquet garni* if you like. Cover the pan and simmer for three-quarters of an hour. Remove from heat. A *court-bouillon* should be prepared well in advance. When the trout is to be cooked, clean it and put it in the cold *court-bouillon*. Bring to simmering point and poach gently till cooked. Serve with *Hollandaise* sauce or cream sauce.

BRAISING

BRAISED TROUT IN WINE

Fry some rounds of carrot and onion very lightly in butter. Put these in the bottom of a baking dish. Lay the cleaned trout on them, and pour in wine till it comes half-way up the fish. Cover the dish, put it in a moderate oven and cook for thirty or forty minutes, till the trout is tender. Make a thin sauce from the cooking liquor, and serve with vegetables.

COLD TROUT

Any tasty, pink-fleshed trout is good served cold, whether it has been fried, grilled, boiled or braised. It can be eaten with salad and *Mayonnaise* sauce.

Here, it is worth mentioning that there is quite a difference between types of trout. Madame Prunier says that fishermen are very lucky. The trout they catch have often fared well on natural nourishment, and taste far better than any trout bought from a shop. The latter have usually been bred in a fish-farm, and their diet has probably been chosen to make them grow quickly and cheaply, rather than to give them a good flavour.

In general, wild trout can be cooked more simply than trout from a fishmonger's, because they already have plenty of flavour. A pink-fleshed trout can be treated exactly like a salmon or sea-trout, and any of the salmon recipes in cookery books can be used. The following, however, is a recipe which makes *any* trout taste delicious when it is cold.

TRUITES AU CHABLIS

(from Madame Prunier's Fish Cookery Book)

Make a *court-bouillon* with Chablis, and poach the cleaned trout gently in it. When they are cooked, take them out. With the *court-bouillon* and some gelatine, make a jelly. Decorate the trout with tarragon leaves, little sprigs of chervil, white or yolk of hard boiled egg, etc., and cover them deeply with the jelly.

I should like to end this book with a plea—or rather, with some advice. I think it is good advice. But judge for yourself.

Fishing—not only dry-fly fishing but every other sort of fishing as well—depends on clean water. No fish, let alone a trout, will or can live in polluted water. And the law of the land, luckily, forbids anyone to pollute a river or lake, *for any reason whatsoever.* So if anyone pollutes your own fishing, or any fishing you legally lease, you have a perfect right to bring him into court, stop him doing it, and claim damages too.

But would you be able to afford it? The costs of such cases sometimes run into many thousands of pounds. My advice then, is this. Join the Anglers' Co-operative Association—the A.C.A. This organisation exists for the sole purpose of combating water pollution, and does so extremely successfully. It undertakes pollution cases on behalf of its members and indemnifies them against unaffordable costs. You can get full details by writing to the Director, A.C.A., Midland Bank Chambers, Westgate, Grantham, Lincs. NG31 6LE. I have served on the committee of the A.C.A. for many years, and can vouch for the good work it does. Every new member will help not only to protect his own fishing, but also that of others, and also the interests of every man, woman or child who takes pleasure in rivers.

Another body which deserves your support as a trout fisherman is the Salmon and Trout Association. This organisation protects and furthers the interests of all game fishermen, by co-ordinating their views and wishes and representing these wherever the representation can be most effective, such as to Governments. The Association has done particularly useful work in opposing harmful schemes for water abstraction. If you don't know about the Association's work, please find out. Write for details to the Director, Salmon and Trout Association, Fishmongers' Hall, London EC4R 9EL.